1st Edition printed in 2000.

2nd Edition completely revised and amended into 4 books:

Book 1 - ISBN 9781448610068 - 2010
Book 2 - ISBN 9781466405530 - 2011
Book 3 - ISBN 9781466416161 - 2011
Book 4 - ISBN 9781466424609 - 2011

Published by Susan Munzer

This book is the fourth out of a series of four books by the same author.

For more information visit our website:
www.learn2play2learn.com

Dedication

To my parents, Werner and Hanna Briner, who have given their three daughters the best of their heart and strength. My Mom, who has encouraged me to be creative and my Dad, who taught me to be practical and clever with my hands, as well as my two sisters who were part of a great childhood.

To my family, Eric, Marc & Nisha for sharing all these wonderful years. For Eric whose support and dedication to the family has made our lives special and for Marc and Nisha for giving me the opportunity to live a dream and see it fulfilled.

To Oliver, Daniel and Josefine, my first grandchildren and Christina and Dean who have joined our family.

To early childhood education professionals around the globe, who work with dedication and selflessly, and often without adequate compensation, to give children a good foundation in life.

Special Thanks To:

Nisha, for typing the entire book and editing my "Swiss" English text and for being there when I needed her help and encouragement.

Marc, for helping with the creation of the second edition of this book series and for being my special advisor, whose computer expertise, editing help and belief in this book series has been invaluable.

Stuart Dolling, the electronic publishing professional for his valuable help.

All the people who throughout the years have helped me to refine and develop my work through interesting discussions and constructive feedback.

All the wonderful and interesting people I have met through my workshops, whose feedback has encouraged me to pursue this book series.

Susan Munzer

The <u>Learn to Play - Play to Learn</u> Series

This book and DVD series is a set of four illustrated practical guides for parents and caregivers of small children, which examine the relationship between playing and learning and how we as parents and caregivers can support the children in their learning processes.

Have you ever wondered how much children learn as they play, or how important it is for their development to have good toys and the right toys? Did you know how damaging bad toys are, and how easy it is for you to learn to make the right choices?

If children play with the right toys in their very early years, it will get them started on the right path in life. As they learn mental quickness, self-esteem and self-control, to mention just a few, they are later able to master their school years with more interest, and they will have the right foundation for learning.

These are just some of the topics which I am exploring in this book and DVD series. At the same time, I am sharing more than 100 of my self-made toys and 42 story baskets of which 32 I have especially written and created for this series. There are over 450 photographs and 70 patterns with how-to-do explanations. They have made a difference in my children's lives and in the lives of many children of caregivers and parents who I was privileged to teach over the last 40 years. They can make a difference in your child's life, too.

I hope that this series will help you become more creative and more flexible in your teaching style as a parent or as a teacher.

I hope that this series will become a tool for you to teach foundational concept learning that will let children put real building blocks of learning into their development.

I hope that this series will allow you to feel the excitement of knowing that you were instrumental in giving a child a good start in life.

The book and DVD series comprises four books and four DVDs all separately available. The books and DVDs are described in more detail on the next page.

Further educational materials which support the methods and concepts in the <u>Learn to Play - Play to Learn</u> series are available through our webpage:

www.learn2play2learn.com

This series is made up of four books. Each part comprises both a book and a DVD film. The book explains the concepts with pictures, patterns and text and the DVD film supplements the book by illustrating the concepts via a filmed presentation with the author.

The four books are:

- Book 1 - Educational Storytelling
- Book 2 - Story Baskets
- Book 3 - Math and Science
- Book 4 - Puppets and Empathy

Book 1 - Educational Story Telling

This book looks at what children learn as they play and as they hear stories. We look at questions like: How do we bring out childrens individuality, potential and talent? How do we reduce TV time and fill it with great learning? This is a great parent and teacher support and provides ideas which are much loved by the children!

Book 2 - Story Baskets

In this book we introduce 25 story baskets in words and pictures. With the Story Basket method we learn to be flexible, use any materials at hand to entertain, delight and teach children. Much effort is put on virtues and empathy which can be used to provide great lessons on good morale. This is an all time childrens favorite!

Book 3 - Math and Science

In this book we introduce ways of teaching math and science by concept learning in order to build a solid foundation for later school years. We discuss how to choose and make toys and exercises for hands on learning with easy to find materials. Discover nature as a great teacher. Included are 9 story baskets focussed on math and science.

Book 4 - Puppets and Empathy

In this book we look at puppets and how they can be used in education. Children can easily connect and relate to puppets which allows puppets to present amazing opportunities to teach virtues and empathy. We look at different varieties of puppets and show how to make some yourself. Included are 7 more story baskets focussed on empathy.

All four books include do-it-yourself projects with patterns and helpful tips.

Puppets and Empathy
TABLE OF CONTENTS

Puppets and Empathy
Story Baskets:

INTRODUCTION

Here the magic box arrives with the clowns!

PUPPETS

If you work with children and you surround yourself with a few puppets, you will make friends quickly. Children may be skeptical or shy towards you, but with a puppet you can start a conversation more easily and the ice is broken quickly. The most valuable puppets are the ones you make yourself. It can be an old sock with two buttons for eyes or a paper bag with some paint on it. It is the interaction, tone of voice and mimicking that counts. You can have the most beautiful and expensive puppet, but if you show no enthusiasm and have no interest, something will be missing. The most important thing about homemade puppets is that you feel special towards it. The children will pick up on this. If you love the children and sincerely want this contact, then it will work. Children are easily entertained and are not demanding at all. They would find it enormously funny if you would make a puppet from Daddy's sock that had lost its mate. How can a sock find its mate without eyes? A puppet can become a special friend who watches every evening to see if the teeth have been brushed properly. We do not need to be professionals or be specially trained, we can just use a puppet one on one or with a group of children for simple conversations or teaching activities. It is however, a lot of fun to get into making your own puppet shows by yourself or with a friend. I often did puppet shows when the children were little and we had a lot of fun, even with the preparing. We have done them from behind chairs, behind tipped tables, with blankets across a doorway and with a self-made Puppet Theater. Just set it up and the children will be game. When we got together as families, we would make a Puppet Show so adults could have a quiet moment. However, the adults always ended up at the show too. The most fun part is to watch children as they participate and interact.

There are many different types of puppets. For puppet shows you can make hand puppets, stick puppets or string puppets. The children could make a puppet theater with a box for finger puppets. These are always easy to handle and are loved by the children. A stick puppet is any character made out of wood, a stuffed toy etc, and mounted on a stick. With this puppet, you do not have to move any parts of the body, they just move across the stage as they are, unless you have some wiggly ears, legs or arms.

I will introduce some of my puppets with photos and patterns. Most of them are easy to make and only need scrap materials. You will probably know someone who has scrap fabric, wool, fur or leather etc.

Puppets in this section:

1. Hand Puppets
2. Finger Puppets
3. Cone Puppets
4. Broomstick Dolls
5. Squeeze my Cheeks Puppets
6. Tumble Fritz
7. Glove Puppets
8. Dress Doll
9. Hobby Horse
10. Other toys in my Puppet Box

1. Hand Puppets: Hand puppets are great to make because you only need one pattern to make many different ones. However, there are many different ways to make puppets. I used to make them with paper mache. This however, takes much too long because you have to let things dry between steps. An easy way to make puppets is with Styrofoam balls. If you prepare all the material, you can make one in two to three hours. You need:

- Stretchy piece of fabric for the head part.
- Fabric for the body part.
- A piece of card board to make a a cone over your finger.
- A 2 ½" (6 cm) Styrofoam ball.
- Felt for the hands.
- Depending on what character, you need eyes, ears, hair, pieces of ribbon etc.

How to Make the Puppet:

- Cut the main body part double and lengthen the pattern 2" (5 cm), so that your arm is covered when you play. All around, add 3/8" (1 cm) for the seams.
- Cut the headpiece double and add seams.
- Cut two hands double from felt. Don't add seams.
- Sew all four-hand pieces separately onto the arms (as shown in pattern) so that the seams are on the inside.
- Pin the two body pieces with the hands attached together. Sew by machine or by hand. Do the same to the headpiece and leave the straight part open. I usually sew the felt hands together by hand. Your thumb and index finger will be inside the hands, so make sure that they will fit.
- Cut the cardboard cone and glue together to fit over your pointer finger.
- Make a hole in your Styrofoam ball with a pencil to fit your cone. Glue the cone inside the Styrofoam ball.
- Pull the head fabric over the Styrofoam ball, put glue on the cardboard cone and drape the fabric nicely around it & tie it down with a few rounds of thread. You can change the shape of the head by putting some stuffing in with the ball before you glue the fabric down.
- Decorate the head and sew onto the body part.

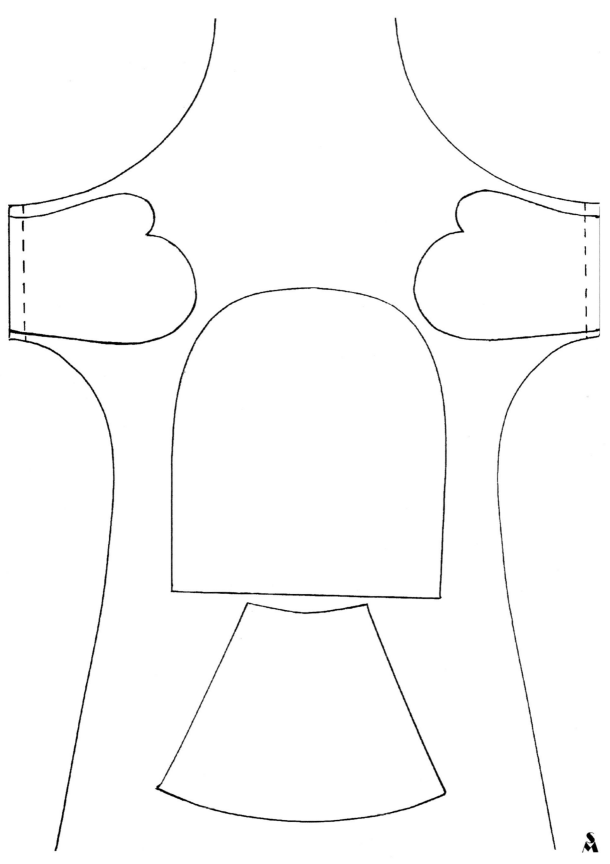

(Note: enlarge pattern by 20%)

2. Finger Puppets: You can sew, knit or crochet a finger puppet. You don't have to be an expert sewer as you can easily sew two small felt pieces together. One little finger puppet can be very special for a child. Children can even sew these together themselves. It could be a good sewing exercise for Kindergarten children. With only a few little pieces of felt, a little hair and eyes, they become alive on your finger. You can even do them as you watch TV (if you must). Finger puppets are very suitable for finger games; five little ducks, five little sharks, five green and speckled frogs or five little monkeys etc. You can do these finger games by taking five children and letting them all have one puppet. Then as you play the game, children go back to their place as this one gets lost or that one was jumping on the bed. At the end of the game, the children can bring the puppet to a friend and the game can begin again. Look in your books or in the library for finger poems, and you will see that many are suitable.

You can make sets for your child's preschool teacher and add the poem to it. These sets make beautiful little gifts and cost about 25 cents to make. Make them for craft fairs or bazaars or bring them to a sick child. I made sets for two children that were going on a long airplane trip. I wrapped them and told them that they were not to be opened until they were on the plane. I did this while teaching preschool. Their dad was a police officer. One day I was running late and was driving rather fast to school. I saw him too late...but he was discreetly and purposely looking the other way! I wanted to repay his kindness!!

When you look at the photos of the finger puppets, you will see that it needs very little to dress them up. Be confident that you can do it. The color will do most of the job. If you want to make a pig, take pink felt and it will only need eyes, a nose and a snout. You will be amazed how little is required. They never have to be perfect. In fact, the ones with the most character are the lopsided ones!

It is nice to have a finger puppet stand (see pattern). All you have to do is take a square piece of ½" (12 mm) plywood or other wood, and drill five holes the size of your pieces of dowel. Three pieces of the dowel are longer; cut them 4" (10 cm); the other two pieces in the front are 3" (7 ½ cm). If they are staggered like this, you will be able to see the puppets in the back better. I use ¼" (6 mm) dowel. I have used the Finger Puppet pattern below for The Three Bears story (big, middle and small), but you can use any of the sizes. The smallest pattern is perfect for the children's small fingers.

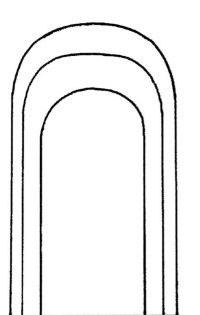
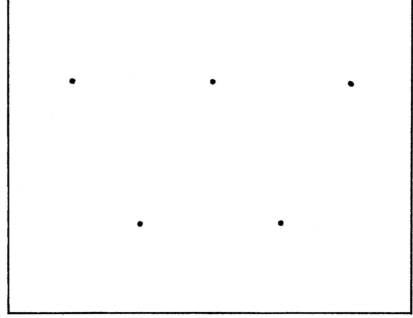

3. Cone Puppets:

Cone puppets are great for personal contact with the children. Children are fascinated because they move so magically and they can hide inside the cone and play peek-a-boo. As you move the stick, the puppet turns to look at the children or hops up and down. Children will clean up faster if you walk around with the puppet inside the cone and tell them

that the puppet will visit when all is cleaned up. The puppet can go around after and see if everyone did a good job. The cone puppet can ask questions, tell a story or introduce a poem or a song.

• If you follow these simple steps, you will be able to make your own cone puppet.

• Cut out double fabric for the body and the head. Add 3/8" (1 cm) for the seams. When sewing, leave an opening at the top and the bottom of the body piece. For the headpiece, leave it open on the straight part. I used stretchy fabrics, preferably velour and I like to use plain colors.

• The cardboard cone is the exact size as in the pattern. Drill holes every half-inch on both sides. The thickness of the cardboard is so that it is strong, but still workable for bending without breaking. Mine is a little less than 1/16" (a bit more than one mm).

• Work cardboard gently over the edge of the table until you get a cone. Do not break the cardboard. Sew the cone together with white string in a shoelace fashion.

- Cut the fabric to cover the cone, add seams to the pattern and sew together. Choose a nice pattern that goes well with the color of the puppet. Put glue onto the cardboard cone. Do not put glue closer than one inch from the top, otherwise the fabric gets hard and it gets difficult to sew the puppet on. Pull the fabric on and smooth out the creases.

Try to work quickly before the glue dries. Put aside to dry.

- Paint stick and let dry.
- Put a 2" (5 cm) Styrofoam ball   into the headpiece and add stuffing if desired to shape the head.
- Poke the stick (18" or 46 cm long and 5/16" or 8 mm diameter) into the Styrofoam ball about 3/4 through, take the stick out and put a lot of glue into the hole and around the fabric. Put the stick back in, arrange the head fabric around the stick and tie it around the stick all the way down the neck.
- Finish the head according to character - eyes, ears, hair etc.
- Put the body onto the stick and sew around the neck with a few stitches.
- Put the stick through the cone and pin the puppet to the edge of the cone fabric (edge of cardboard). Sew together (only the fabrics). Glue a ribbon around the edge of the one (cardboard) to make it look finished.
- Glue a bead to the end of the stick.

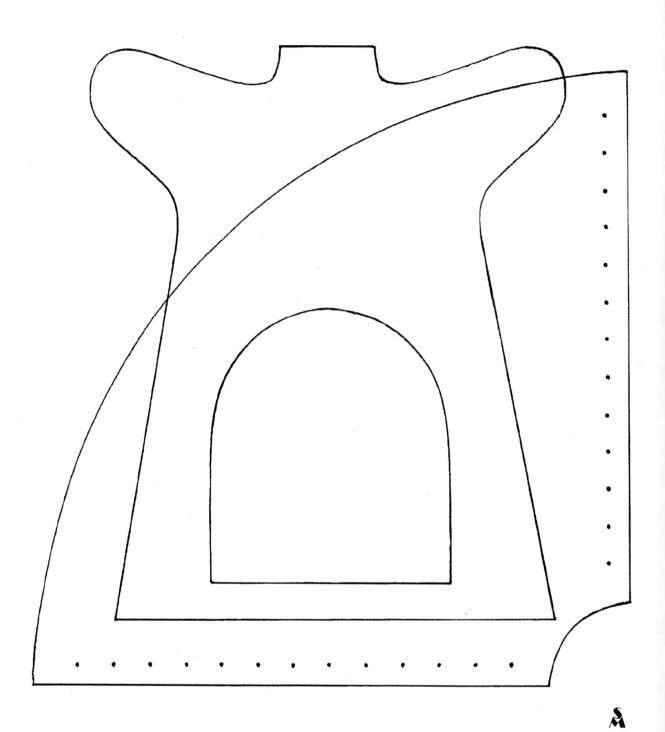

Note: enlarge pattern by 20%

4. Broomstick Dolls: Broomstick dolls can be made in any size that you want by changing the thickness of the dowel or the length. You can tailor make them to your doll house furniture or for any story where you need people. They are very strong and they stand well. I have used them in a few stories (you can find them in the pictures). I will give you the dimensions for the broomstick clown:

• Take one piece of an old broomstick (you could even cut a piece off your new broom.) The length of my clown is 4" (10 cm) with a diameter of 7/8 to 1" (22 to 25 mm). Make a small groove for the neck by whittling or by grinding with a file or use a grinding machine with a small disc. Drill a hole about 3/8" (1 cm) below the groove for the arms. Use a 7/32" (5 mm) drill.

• Sand well and paint. To make polkadots, I dip a new eraser from the end of a pencil into paint.

• Arms: Sew a small fabric tube with a length of 4" (10 cm) width 5/8" (1½ cm) finished size. To turn inside out, attach a string on a large needle at one end, feed through the tube and pull through. Next, pull the needle still attached to the sleeve, through the hole.

• Hands: Turn the ends of the sleeves in so that it doesn't fray. Next, attach beads by sewing through the hole of the bead.

• To make hair, crochet a few lines of wool, iron with steam, let dry and unravel. Glue hair, cap and pompom into place. Fix a frill around the neck.

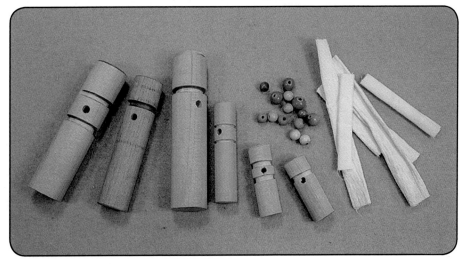

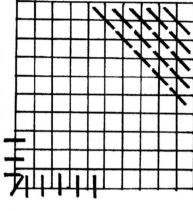

5. Squeeze my Cheeks Puppets: These puppets are very easy to work for children. Some of you may remember these puppets that people make with a chocolate kiss inside. They are also often made for Christmas decorations or found at craft fairs. They are fun to make with children 8-10 year old. They are made with a plastic canvas, that you can buy in craft stores. Here is how to make them:

• Cut out plastic canvas squares that have ten holes on each side. Each puppet needs three squares of 10. Cover them with wool as shown in the drawing, leaving the edges bare. Sew together the first two squares on two sides to make a cone. Next, add the third square onto one of the tips of the open cone (also sewn onto two sides). When you sew them always make two to three stitches in the corners. Often I cut the corners off the plastic canvas squares before I cover them with wool so that the corners do not look too pointy. Don't cut corners on the side, that's where you squeeze!

• Dress up with pieces of felt, pompoms or googli-eyes etc.

• If you sew the third square on wrong, you will get a fish.

• You can have a few squeeze the cheek characters hanging from a stick between two chairs for the children to play with.

• The three bears are Papa (11 holes), Mama (9 holes), and Baby bear (7 holes). Felt eyes are just as nice as googli-eyes.

• This type of puppet is ideal for the "Princess and the Frog" story because the frog can put the ball in its mouth.

• Use this puppet to hide little messages in the mouth and give to people.

18

6. Tumble Fritz: This little clown can tumble down the ironing board all by himself. Put a towel or some other non-slippery fabric on the ironing board and little Fritz will tumble down. Inside this character is a paper roll with a steel ball from a ball bearing. The weight from the steel ball pulls the character along and makes him flip. Children love this little guy. I kept him for birthdays and would give it to them as a special toy to play with all day long at school. They could let other children play with him, or they could hog him all to themselves. All the children always wanted to take him home with them, but I would have to explain that we need him for the next birthday and he would come reluctantly out of the child's pocket. It is nice to have something just for a special day. (Directions are as follows:)

• Put the body pattern on the felt so that the fold is along the upper arm line. You do not have to add a seam. You can make the hands and shoes a different color from the body. Cut open the neck opening for the paper roll. Sew together with small winding stitches by hand, or if you prefer, you can use the sewing machine.

• Cut out head pieces and sew together.

• The paper roll is 2 3/8" (6 cm) long. The opening is 1 ¼" (3 cm). Most gift wrapping paper is on this size of rolls. The steel ball is 1" (2 ½ cm) big. To prepare the paper roll, cut 2 circles of strong, thin fabric. Glue them on each side of the paper roll with the steel ball inside. Hold in place with two elastics. Cut a strip of heavy paper 2 3/8" (6 cm) wide and 11" (28 cm) long. Glue this around the paper roll when it is dry but take the elastics off first. You will get around about two times. The additional paper will give it extra strength together with the glue.

• Now you can assemble Fritz and glue everything together. Stick a little bit of fur under the cap and sew a small bell on the tip of the hat. Do not use too much glue so the cap does not get too hard. Fritz doesn't tumble with a hard cap. Draw or paint on a happy face.

19

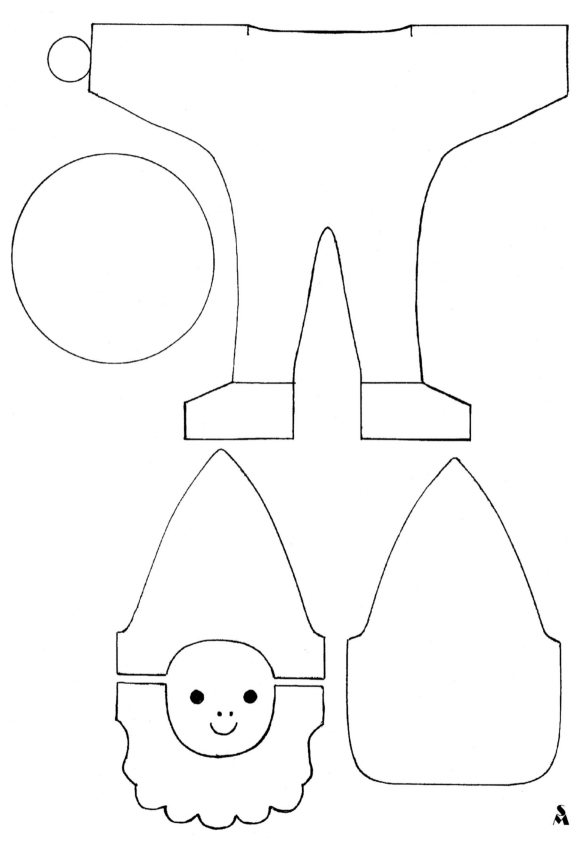

Note: enlarge pattern by 20%

7. Glove Puppets: Take a garden glove and find a plastic container that is small enough to fit the glove, but large enough to fit your hand. Cut out the bottom of the container. Punch holes all around the bottom of the container with a small hole punch. Fit the glove over the container and sew on through the holes. Decorate figures with pompoms, pieces of felt, bow ties, and eyes, according to what character you are making. I always sew everything on very well so that the children cannot pull the pieces off. You can make them all the same or all different. By not showing the whole glove, it looks as though the characters are just peeking out of the basket. When you move your fingers, they look as if they are alive. Here is a little song that goes with my basket of puppies:

Five Little Puppy Dogs

Five little puppy dogs in a basket so snug,
Feeling very tired and settling down on their rug.
The first one gets itchy and catches a flea,
The second one gets tickled and is all giggly,
The third one is stretching himself and is yawning,
The fourth one just closed his eyes and is snoring,
The fifth little doggy is dreaming of food,
He loves to eat something very very good.

21

8. Dress Doll: This toy is marvelously simple to make and the children love to play with it because they can dress up the doll very easily. Dressing up regular dolls can be difficult. Small children often have a hard time putting the arms in the sleeves or closing the buttons. I usually make two shapes, one like a dress and one like a jumpsuit. You can make them two sided, with one side being a person with black hair and on the other side a person with blond hair with a different colored background. When children play with the fabric pieces, they can match colors and see which side of the fabric looks nicer. Have many different types of fabric squares in different colors and patterns; flannel, satin, corduroy, velvet, silk, cotton etc. Have a few strips of ribbon and lace to add as borders and belts.

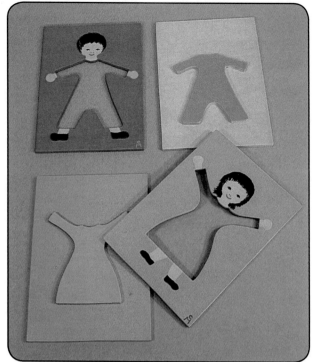

• If you want to make one boy and one girl, precut four squares from ¼" (6 mm) plywood and trace the pattern on two squares. Cut the dress and the jumpsuit with a drill start. I always cut about 1/32" (1 mm) of the wood off all around the dress and the jumpsuit to give extra space for the fabric. Sand all the pieces well.

• Paint all six pieces with plain color. Paint head, hands and feet on the pieces that have the holes. When the paint has dried, glue the dress and jumpsuit part onto the whole plywood pieces. Center them by putting the top and bottom part together. By doing this, you will see exactly where the pieces have to go. The figures are dressed by simply putting a piece of fabric between the boards.

• Cut a variety of fabrics, 7" by 5 ½" (18 x 14 cm). Use the children's old discarded clothing for fabric. A favorite piece of clothing that they have outgrown will be extra special. I have found heart tins that I used for this toy. It is smaller and can easily be taken on trips. It is like bringing your doll with a suitcase of clothing along on a trip!

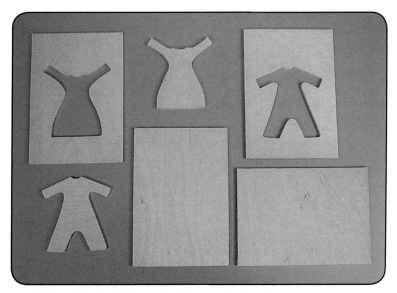

9. Hobby Horse

1. Glue and nail the little board to the end of the stick. Sand the stick for smoothness, you don't want slivers.
2. Stuff the front part of the sock. Instead of making it long and skinny, try to stuff width into the sock.
3. Put the stick with the little board inside the sock (heel).
4. Finish stuffing the sock, especially around the little board and the whole neck, right down to the edge of the sock.
5. Put a string with a gather stitch around the opening of the sock, pull closed, glue and tie everything together.
6. Sew harness bands, ears, eyes and nose with pieces of leather, felt or fabric. Put a few bells on, children love the sound.
7. Glue or stitch the mane on.
8. Have a ride!

Materials Needed for the Hobby Horse

You might want to change a few things depending on the age of the child and the size of the sock, etc.

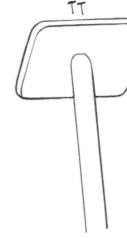

Stick: Dowel 1" (2.5 cm) thick - 3 to 4 feet (90-120 cm) long.

Little Board: Plywood 2 1/2" x 3 1/2" ((6 x 9 cm) + 2 nails.

Sock: Find a fuzzy sports sock, men's size.

Mane: Use fur, shredded stocking, wool, unraveled sweater, etc.

Ears, Eyes & Nose: Use pieces of leather, fabric, double felt, buttons or googli-eyes.

Harness: Use strips of leather or decorative bands.

Bells: Sew on a few bells, children love the sound.

This is a great project for children to help. The horse will become more special to them as they feel an ownership with it.

27

Other Toys in my Puppet Box

1. Bead Dolls

Take large beads to make little people. I have ten on a little stand as a counting game.

"1 little, 2 little, 3 little children,
4 little, 5 little, 6 little children,
7 little, 8 little, 9 little children,
10 little children play.

10 little, 9 little, 8 little children,
7 little, 6 little, 5 little children,
4 little, 3 little, 2 little children,
1 little child alone."

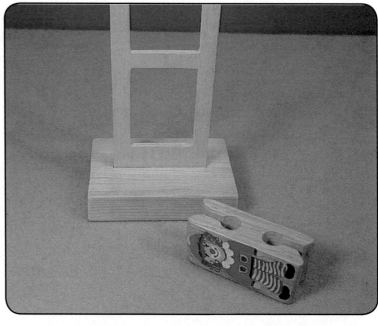

2. & 3. Peggy Man and Clown on a Ladder

They are climbing down little pegs while the other flip flops down the ladder.

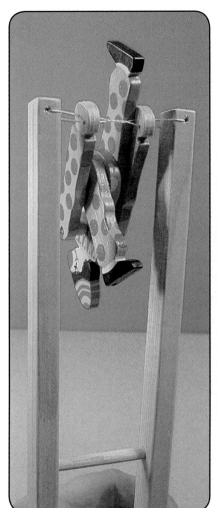 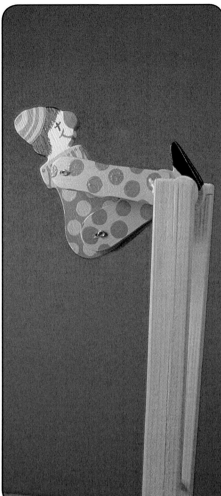 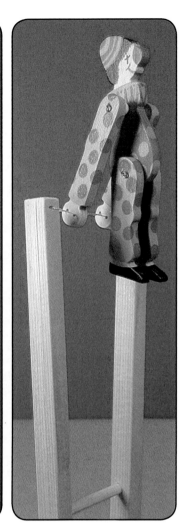

4. Athletic Clown

A clown who magically does acrobatic exercises on 2 strings as you squeeze the two sticks.

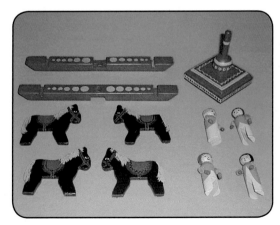

5. Merry-Go-Round

Children take apart a merry-go-round, (11 pieces).

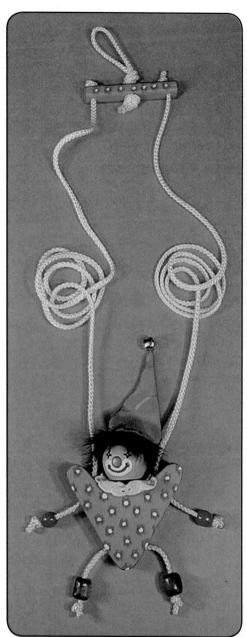

6. Climber

Alternately pull on the strings to make the clown climb up.

7. & 8. Pecking Chickens & Parrot

Birds peck food by swinging the toy in a circular motion.

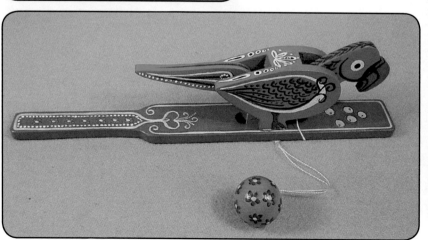

30

Conclusion Without Words...

Story Baskets for Puppets & Empathy

Here are the different aspects of learning in each of the individual stories.

Story	Aspect of Learning	Theme	Emotional and Moral Value
1. The Magic Land **A**	Science Social Virtues	Teamwork Fishing Show and Tell	Sharing Listening to Advice To Teach a Lesson
2. The Little Old Lady **A**	Science Math Safety Nutrition Social	Pond life Laying of Eggs A Good Breakfast	Everyone is Special Scary Night To Feel Cozy
3. Little Red Hen A Fairy Tale	Science Nutrition	Sprouting Seeds Making Flour and Bread	Being Lazy & Greedy Being Industrious Working Hard Getting a Reward Feeling Sorry
4. The Toymaker **A**	Working with Wood Using Tools & Paint	Selecting Wood Making Toys	Delighting Children Making Sad People Happy Finding Solutions
5. Noah's Ark From the Bible	Math Science Social	Counting/Grouping Matching Animal Life Weather/Rainbow	Patience Live Responsibly
6. The Grasshopper and the Bug **A**	Science Job Opportunity Social	Different Animals Teaching Rescuing	Helping Knowing your Talents
7. Meet the King or Queen of Kindness **A**	Social Virtues Empathy	Encouraging Good Behaviour Giving Gifts The Process of having clean Clothes	Make Helping Others a Habit Awarness to Others Needs Feeling Useless

1. The Magic Land

"Give a Little, Take a Little"

Once upon a time, there was a magic land and there was a magic lake. On the magic lake there swam a magic duck. Often 3 little clowns arrived in their magic box, where they liked to play. They would bring some treasures and show each other.

This day one little clown had a stick and said that he could walk across a rope with it, use it for hiking and defend himself against bad dogs! The other little clowns wanted to try it out, hold it and touch it. But the little clown said: "Oh no, this is mine!"

Lay out the red cloth and lake, smuggle 3 fish under lake. Put duck on lake. 3 clowns arrive in box with stick, string and magnet. First clown shows stick.

The second little clown had a really nice rope and said that he could skip with it, hang his washing on it and catch horses with it. The other little clowns wanted to try it out, hold it and touch it. But the little clown said: Oh no, this is mine!"

Second clown shows string.

The third little clown had brought a magnet and said that he could pick up bottle caps with it, put important notes on the fridge and sometimes even find coins with the magnet.

Third clown shows magnet.

The other little clowns found it very interesting and wanted to try it out, hold it and touch it. But the little clown said: "Oh no, this is mine!"

The little duck who was listening was very surprised that the little clowns did not know how to share! So he went up to them with a great idea. He said: "Did you know that there are magic fish in the lake? If you had a fishing rod you could catch some!"

Little duck goes over to clowns.

The little clowns were very sad, one said: "I only have a stick!" The other one said: "I only have a rope!" And the last one said: "I only have a magnet!"

Clowns assemble fishing rod. Hold onto lake fabric as the magnet attaches to fish, and gets pulled out.

The little duck said if you put your heads together you will see that you could make a fishing rod with these things. And that's what they did. They each caught a beautiful fish and they realized that there is magic in sharing.

You can slide the fish to the edge and pull it out, practice a few times.

And they lived happily ever after.

It looks like magic.

It is a very special moment when if like magic the fish who are under the lake fabric attach to the magnet and are actually on the fising rod as you pull them out. Children are fascinated.

Materials Needed for The Magic Land

This story is very flexible, you don't necessarily need clowns, you can take any 3 critters -- a chicken, a cow and a pig, etc. You always need a stick, a string and a magnet. Critters can arrive in a car, on a carpet or in a sleigh, etc.

Fabric: Any color

Lake: A piece of fabric that works with the magnet. Paper will work, too.

Fish: Cut out fun foam fish and put a paperclip on them.

Magnet: Take a fairly strong one, doughnut (with hole) or a horseshoe, so it can easily be attached to a string.

Duck: Take a rubber ducky or any one you can find.

Reflections on The Magic Land

The children find this story very cool, first this amazing idea to make a fishing rod and then actually catching fish with it. So sharing really becomes quite exciting. It is so hard for some children to share their toys, but they want so much to play with someone else's. So there is a conflict. Eventually they learn to give a little and take a little.

That was a really smart duck to entice the clowns with catching a fish to get them to cooperate into making a fishing rod.

It needs a lot of creative thinking and ingenuity for educators working with children to constantly think of non-confrontational ways to guide and lead. Story baskets in general are a great way to address all kinds of issues. Listening to a story is much nicer than feeling that you are being taught a lesson or that you have to listen to some advice.

2. The Little Old Lady and her Friends
"Everyone is Special"

Once upon a time there was a meadow. On that meadow there was a pond where a beautiful duck lived. Around the pond there were some flowers and if you looked really closely, you could see a nest. Further down, there was a little log house where the little old lady lived. She was very happy and did not need many things. She had a bed, a table, and a few dishes, but most important she had two baskets. One was where her two little friends, the dog and the bear would sleep. The other basket she took every morning to the pond to see if the duck had laid an egg for her. She always took her friends along. Without fail, every morning, there was a fresh egg in the nest. The little old lady would get very excited and thank the duck many times for her beautiful and delicious big egg. When she brought the egg home to eat, she would say how wonderful it was. The little dog and the little bear didn't like the fuss she made about those silly eggs. So one night, when everyone was in bed, the little bear and the little dog went down to the pond and decided to become ducks.

They thought that they were not special because they had not given any eggs to the old lady.

Out on the pond where it was very dark, they wished so hard to become ducks that they turned into ducks. When the little old lady woke the next morning, she missed her friends, but thought that they had probably already gone out. When she got to the pond with her basket, she was very surprised to find three ducks and was very excited to have three eggs in the nest. She thanked them many times. On the way home, she looked and called for her friends. But no luck. She went to eat breakfast. After breakfast, she again went out and made a real search for her friends. She looked everywhere, called and cried because she was very sad. This went on for a few days. Everyday she had three eggs and everyday she missed her friends. She didn't really need three eggs, one was just right. The bear and dog out on the pond didn't like being ducks anymore. It was wet and damp everywhere and they longed for their cozy basket in the long, dark and scary nights. So one night, when it was very dark, the bear and dog wished so hard to be themselves again that they turned into a bear and dog again. Were they glad! They snuck into the house and into their cozy basket. In the morning everyone was very happy, they hugged and hugged and they then knew that they were very special too. They didn't have to lay an egg to be special. And they lived happily ever after.

- Lay out green fabric, pond flowers and nest as you speak.
- Lay out 4 logs, little old lady, bed, table, 1 dish & 2 baskets.
- Smuggle eggs into nest and introduce bear and dog.
- The 3 take basket and get egg.
- Put egg into basket.
- Put egg into plate.
- All 3 go to bed and dog and bear sneak out.

- Get children to close eyes to see how dark it was and exchange with ducks.

- Put 3 eggs into nest.

- Put 3 eggs into basket.

- Put 1 egg into plate.

- Little old lady looks for friends.

- Get children to close eyes again

- Exchange ducks with bear and dog.

- Hugs for everyone!

Reflections on The Little Old Lady

This is a fairly long story, so you need to practice a bit. The parts where you smuggle the eggs into the nest and exchange the bear, dog and the ducks is a little tricky. Children will get quite involved. I even had one group who would go out and call the bear and dog when they were playing on the playground. This is a very suitable story for children to play by themselves or in pairs. Because there is a house with furniture and quite a few figures, the children will often invent all kinds of action and will like to stay in the story corner for quite a long time. They will play parts of the story and add their own action to it in between. We want them to use their own imagination as much as possible. Sometimes I add a basket with beautiful rocks for the children to put around the pond or for the ducks to sit on in the sun. You can also add trees or bushes. Little lumps of playdough with small branches stuck in them look nice. If they have small leaves it looks very real. Some of the flowers can also be used as lily pads.

With this story we learn that we are all special in our own way. We can point out different talents in each other and learn that we don't have to be good at everything or that we don't have to be like others. We learn that it is o.k. to be ourselves.

The magical part of it makes it very special, of course. Everyone knows that we can't turn into anyone else, but we surely would like to sometimes. We all have our wishes and dreams. However, it is really quite okay to be ourselves. We feel much more stable to know that we can be ourselves and that with our uniqueness, we can contribute to the group. When we do this story, we as parents and caregivers should think of well-deserved compliments we can give. Especially to children who often go unnoticed, it might be the only compliment that child received in a long time. The effect of an encouraging remark is much better than scolding.

> Mark Twain once said:
>
> **"I can live sixty days on one compliment."**

A compliment is a nice gift,
when given in love and honesty,
without flattery, sarcasm or teasing.

Materials needed for Little Old Lady and Her Friends

Fabric: Green cloth 24" by 24" (60 cm x 60 cm)

Pond: Cut out of wood, fabric or paper. I also found blue shiny plastic placemats that were perfect for this.

Flowers: As many as you want. Make your own, or take real daisy heads or other flowers.

Nest: A patch of real, completely dried moss, glued onto a round piece of cardboard with lots of glue.

Eggs: 3 plastic eggs, or 3 beans, or 3 eggs made out of play dough.

House: Four sticks for logs 9" long (23 cm).

Furniture: Very simple things made yourself or taken from a dollhouse.

Dishes: I used acorn bowls.

Little old lady: Take any little person, put on a scarfe.

3 ducks, 1 bear, 1 dog: Cut out 1/2" (12 mm) plywood or make them out of modeling clay. You could also insert a piece of dowel into a finger puppet to get standup puppets.

3. The Little Red Hen
"Teamwork is Fun"

Once upon a time there was a village and there were 5 houses. In the first house lived the little red hen (LRH) with her babies. In the second house lived a dog and in the third and fourth houses lived a cat and a pig.

The fifth house was a mill where the Miller lived.

One day the LRH found some grains of wheat. She was very happy and decided to plant them. She asked her friends, the dog, the cat and the pig for help, but they were all tired, busy, lazy, going for a walk, bathing in a puddle or sleeping in the hay, etc.

So the LRH decided to do it all by herself. She had a nice box by her door where she planted the wheat. She checked every day. Many days passed and in the summer the wheat was ripe and golden.

The LRH asked her friends to help her reap the wheat. But again everybody had excuses. (Be inventive). So the LRH worked all by herself with the babies at her side.

Then she asked her friends to help her take the wheat to the mill to be ground, but everybody had excuses again. So she went all by herself.

The Miller ground the wheat into flour and gave the LRH a nice big bag of flour.

The LRH asked her friends to help her make the dough to make some bread, but again everybody was busy and lazy. She and the babies went into their house to make the bread. Soon there was a lovely smell coming from the house and all the friends started sniffing the air.

The LRH came out and asked her friends who would help her eat this bread. Now everybody came running and wanted some of this fine bread.

But the LRH put out the blanket, put the bun in the middle and sat her babies around it and said to her friends:

"You didn't help me plant or reap or grind or bake and so now we are going to eat this bread all by ourselves!"

And by golly they did and lived happily ever after.

Lay out cloth. Set out houses.
Set in front hen and babies.
Set out dog, cat and pig.
Set out Miller.
Sprinkle a few grains of wheat.
LRH finds them.
Hen talks to friends.

Plants wheat in the pot.

Stick real full grown wheat into pot.

Hen talks to friends.

Hen takes wheat to the mill.
Miller goes behind mill with wheat.
He brings out a bag of flour.
Hen talks to friends.

Hen and babies go behind house with bag of flour.
Dog, cat and pig come closer.

Hen and babies come with a blanket and the bun.

Dog, cat and pig watch how the others eat.

40

Materials needed for The Little Red Hen

Fabric: Any color.

Houses: My puzzle is optional, made with 1/2" (12mm) plywood. Paint houses on both sides, put details only on the front. Make sure you know which side the front is when you paint, otherwise the puzzle doesn't fit. You can make houses with Lego or blocks.

Animals: Cut from 1/2" (12mm) plywood or find any others. You can use other animals too -- a cow, a horse and a rooster, etc.

3 Chicks: Find the little fluffy ones at Easter.

Miller: Any little man with white apron add a white sack.

Grain: Small bag with a few kernels of wheat and a few real ears of wheat. Collect in the Fall. You can find them in a craft store in the dried flower section.

Container: With sand to plant the wheat kernels, then the green sprouts and the ears.

Blanket: Small piece of fabric.

Bun: Produce miraculously a fresh bun to share with children.

Other: Brown paper for puddle, soft mat or moss to snooze on.

Reflections on The Little Red Hen

Children love stories of repetition, they know what is coming and that feels good. That's why children love to hear a story over and over again. They can build true memory. Our time seems to over-stimulate and over-crowd a child's day with too much activity, information and adult related content. So it is a real pleasure for a child to sit quietly in a cozy corner to do a well known and loved story with someone they love. This story of cause is a helping and sharing story -- but what I noticed when I watch the children is how frustrated they get with all the so-called friends that don't want to help. So at the end of the story I ask: Who would have liked to help the Little Red Hen? This is a great moment of relief because everybody would have liked to help. Then I say that I was very happy that they all wanted to be good friends and that we were going to ask the Little Red Hen if she would like to share her bun with the children. It is great to see how everybody eats this little piece of bread proudly and how everybody thinks that this is the best bread they ever had.

It is a marvelous story on planting, growing and making bread. Every step can be expanded on and can be a lesson in itself. When you read the book to the children, you will see that everybody has a much better understanding of the run of events and they will see all the details behind the picture with their creative mind. This is reinforcing and building memory.

It is a story that needs a lot of preparation but it is well worth it. I usually use my hand grain mill to grind some of the wheat into flour with the children. Then we make the dough with a bit of water and yeast -- however we still use the finished bun. This is a great story for dramatizing as well.

4. The Toymaker
"Find a Happy Solution"

Once upon a time there was a Toymaker. He had a nice workshop where he was very happy and whistled often as he worked. He had a beautiful piece of wood and decided to make a Mama Doll.

Lay out cloth, put a box on top and cover with other cloth.

He took his tools: a saw, a hammer and a file and started to work. Soon the Mama Doll was ready to be painted, so he brought out his paints and brushes. He worked for a long time and liked the doll very much when it was finished. It had bright colors and looked very pretty standing on the shelf.

Put on work apron and whistle a tune. Show children piece of wood. Bring out tools. Bring out paints and brushes.

The next morning when the Toymaker came to his workshop he said "Good Morning" to the doll and noticed that she was crying. "Why are you sad," the man asked? "I am a Mama Doll and I would very much like to have a child," she replied. So the Toymaker carved another doll and when it was finished it looked like a smaller Mama Doll. They were both very happy.

Show children finished doll.

Put on the box.

The next morning when the Toymaker came to his workshop his new Mama Doll was crying too, and wanted a child. So he made another one.

Take out next size doll.

Repeat with each additional doll you have and then...when the Toymaker came to his workshop and the littlest Mama Doll wanted a baby too -- he thought really hard. What could he do? The doll was getting so small, he would be unable to make them even smaller. He decided to make a little boy because everybody knows that little boys don't have babies. The little boy was very happy and the doll family lived happily ever after.

Take out next size doll.

In the last doll that can be opened have a little boy.

Take out little boy.

Materials needed for The Toymaker

<u>Fabric:</u>   Any color

<u>Tools:</u>   A hammer, a saw and paints with brushes.

<u>Stacking Dolls:</u> Hopefully you will find one. Take out last solid doll and replace with a little boy. Attach a bead on a piece of dowel and paint.

<u>Optional:</u> A work apron for yourself. You can just tie a piece of fabric around your waist. Children like a bit of drama.

Reflections on The Toymaker

There is a whole series of stacking dolls that you can use to make stories. There are animals, different people and a Christmas tree. I even have some politicians and the world (see picture of my collection.) Be creative and use the magic aspect of surprise.

I like to use as much humor as I can in my stories. It is great to laugh together and have some fun. It is very important though, to teach children that something is only funny if it is funny for everybody. We don't make fun on someone else's expense. Children do find it funny that all of a sudden the little boy comes out.

You either want to move on very quickly and not let children ask too many questions about where babies come from -- or you can use it as an opportunity to talk about it -- especially in a family situation. Be prepared!

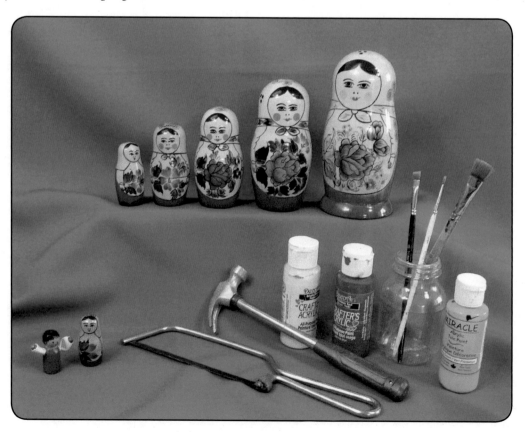

All these stacking dolls help with counting, sizing and sorting.

5. Noah's Ark
"Live Responsibly"

Once upon a time there was a country and in this country lived a good man. His name was Noah. One day God told Noah to build an ark and Noah did. He used some big, long pieces of wood for the bottom part, and he built it up with many other pieces of wood. There was a big door in the side and a big ramp leading up to the boat. Then God told Noah to take animals into the ark, and Noah did. He took in two of every kind. He took in elephants and giraffes, camels and bears, horses, cows and donkeys, sheep, pigs and beavers, dogs, geese and bunnies, alligators and doves. Then God told Noah to bring in his family, and Noah did. God told Noah to close the doors because he would send a great, big rain that would not stop for a long time, a rain that would flood all the wickedness out of the world. So Noah did.

- Lay out green fabric, bring out Noah.
- Build an ark with blocks.

- Bring in all the animals.

- Bring in Noah's family.
- Close door.

Then it rained and it rained. It rained for forty days and forty nights. The whole countryside started to be covered in water and soon Noah's ark started to float. Everyone in the ark was safe. When finally the rain stopped and the water started to go down, the ark came to rest on a mountain. Everyone inside the ark was getting impatient and wanted to go outside. So Noah sent out one of the doves to go see if the plants and the grass had grown back yet. Everyone was excited to see the dove return with a twig in its beak and soon Noah opened the door. All the animals and all of Noah's family came outside and enjoyed the sunshine. As the animals were going away two by two, there was a beautiful big rainbow in the sky. Then God said, "this rainbow is a sign for you that I will never send a great flood again. God told Noah to make a new world, and Noah did. And they lived happily for a long long time.

- All children make motion of raining with arms and hands. Cover green with blue patches of fabric.

- Start taking away blue fabric. Dove flies away and brings twig back, open door, animals come out

- Two children make a rainbow.

Reflections on Noah's Ark

Noah's ark is a story from the Bible and can be found in the Old Testament in Genesis 5:28-9:29. This story in its simplified version has fascinated children and adults for a long time. Children love to set up the animals, find the two that go together, make little rows or fit them all into the boat that they can build with blocks. Some animals are exactly the same, while others are different being male and female. This can be a bit of a challenge. I have also made some looking down and the mate standing up. In this way, children can't just match the shapes, they have to see what it is first. I did not paint these animals. They look nice in just plain wood. This makes it more difficult to find the pairs as well because there are no colors to match. When children play by themselves, they group animals into farm animals, wild animals etc.

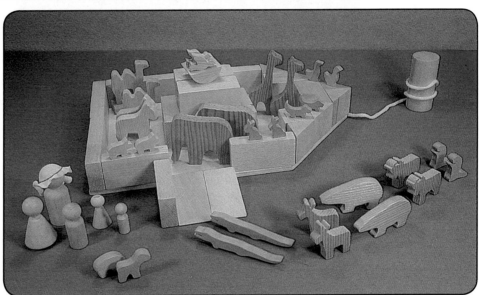

With this story, you can really involve the children. They can pretend to hammer along with Noah as he starts to build the ark. The children can then make the motion of raining. You can have a moment of complete silence to see if the rain has completely stopped. Also, all the children can make the sun as the door opens so that all the animals can enjoy the sun as they emerge from the ark.

Before you start the story, you can talk about the **rainbow**, and how you need one at the end of the story. You can practice with the children, always two children facing each other and holding hands together. Then you can determine with the children, who is dressed the most colorful and choose two children. When the time comes and you need your rainbow, you will have it. Children love the theatrical input that they can give.

We can talk about how important it is that we do our part to keep the world from becoming wicked. God saved Noah because he listened to God. We can't always do what we want, we have to live our lives responsibly.

Materials Needed for Noah's Ark

<u>Fabric:</u> Green 24" by 24" (60 x 60 cm) Wavy strips of blue fabric to cover the green piece by piece.

<u>Ark:</u> An assortment of blocks suitable to build an ark in the proper size according to the animal size. You can have a piece of plywood in the shape of a boat so the children have something to start with.

<u>Animals:</u> Same as the photo: the thickness of the wood is as follows:
½" (13 mm) for elephant and giraffe.
7/16" (11 mm) for cow, bear, donkey and camel.
5/16" (8 mm) for beaver, sheep, pig, alligator.
¼" (6 mm) for bunny, goose, dog and dove.
I have taken scraps of pieces of molding. Anything that you find in these approximate thicknesses will work. You can enlarge the patterns and get bigger animals. The little ones are more suitable to play with on the table. Larger ones would be more suitable for floor play with bigger blocks.

<u>Noah and his Family:</u> Little wooden people in different sizes, or broomstick dolls. I left mine plain like the animals, except for Noah had a white cloth and a band around his head.

<u>Twig:</u> Any twig with a few green leaves on it. I would make sure it is not poisonous because the children might pretend to be a dove and put it in their mouths.

<u>Rainbow:</u> Two children (see Reflections).

Note: Enlarge pattern by 20%

6. The Grasshopper and the Bug

"Knowing Your Talents"

Once upon a time, there was a meadow close to a lake. It was a beautiful place where many animals came to graze, to find honey in the flowers or to drink water in the lake. Out in the lake was an island. It was a big rocky island where nothing could grow. At the edge of the meadow was a beehive where the bees lived. On one side of the meadow lived a grasshopper and on the other side lived a bug. They both didn't like each other. The grasshopper thought that the silly bug couldn't hop and jump with his short legs, and the bug thought that the silly grasshopper couldn't even fly properly with his little wings.

• Lay out fabric, one part blue, one part with small flowers.

• Put out rock.
• Put out beehive.
• Set out grasshopper and bug.

One day, a sad little bunny came to the meadow. It had lost its mother and didn't know how to hop. The grasshopper volunteered to teach the bunny how to hop. Before long, the bunny was hopping around and was very happy. The bug that was watching from the other side of the meadow admired the grasshopper and knew that he could not have showed the bunny how to hop. The very next day, a bee came buzzing across the meadow looking for honey. When she saw the island, she got curious, but when she landed she hurt her wing quite badly on the rocky island. Now she was stranded. The bug that was watching flew to the rescue. The bee climbed on the bugs back and the bug flew her to the beehive where she could see the bee doctor. The grasshopper was very impressed with the bug's rescue mission and knew that he could not have rescued the bee from the island. From that day on, they became friends. They found out that they had many things in common. They drank dewdrops together, watched the sunset and lived happily ever after.

• Bring out bunny.
• Grasshopper and bunny practice hopping.
• Bunny hops away.

• Bee is buzzing over meadow and island.

• Bug rescues bee and brings to hive.

• Grasshopper and bug move towards each other…

Materials Needed for Grasshopper and Bug

Fabric: 24" by 24" (60 x 60 cm). I have taken blue fabric for the lake and 2 strips of green fabric with many very small flowers on it.

Rock: Find a nice big flat rock

Grasshopper & Bug: I found wicker ones - be inventive.

Bee: One yellow and one black pipe cleaner. One piece of 8" wire (20 cm). Small piece of stocking.

Rabbit & Kangaroo: Cut out of ½" (12 mm) plywood.

Beehive: Find a piece of honeycomb or improvise

Reflections on Grasshopper and the Bug

"Everyone Can Do Something Great!"

This is one of those animal stories where you know that something sounds very human. Here we can laugh about it and think we are way beyond such behavior, but are we? We often want others to think that we are great, but inside we feel insecure. By thinking that others are stupid, we hope to make ourselves feel bigger. In real life it is the opposite, we all have to learn to see objectively that we all have strengths and weaknesses. We can admire strengths in each other, and not get smaller ourselves. On the contrary, someone else's strength often makes our lives richer. Guarding our talents, while putting others down makes us very lonely people.

My talents are visual, but someone who is a great listener, even though he does not have much to show for it, still has a very important talent. Everyone can do something great! We have a problem in that we think that we have to fulfill so many requirements in one lifetime. We always see others around us with their talents and so think that we can never keep up. We somehow fail to notice that we are only one human being, with specialized gifts. I am reminded of a garden shop. Everything looks so beautiful, colorful, and spectacular in their multitude. After I buy a few plants to take home, they seem a bit disappointing. We do take pride and joy in every little plant, once we care for them and watch them grow. I believe we have to let our talents grow and take care of them in order to be able to enjoy them.

You can easily change characters in this story. Anything that swims can do the rescue mission to the island. For example; a duck or a turtle will do. You could take a kangaroo to give hopping lessons. The duck or turtle would think how silly it is to have a pocket for a baby rather than a beautiful egg. The kangaroo might think it was very awkward looking how ducks waddle or that turtles crawled so slowly, with absolutely no speed. (This is for our friends in Australia.)

And then there are, like the grasshopper and the bug, some people that always see something negative first. They don't see a good thing when it is right in front of their noses. They harp and grind away on that one little negative thing and don't want to see the 15 positive points.

7. Meet the King or Queen of Kindness
"Make Helping others a Habit"

Hello everybody!

You will not believe this, but I used to be a sock. I had a twin too, and we were very happy together. We belonged to Mr. X. I remember when we were on a shelf in a store and a little boy came along and bought us. The little boy was very proud to buy us. He said we were a Christmas present for his Dad. Soon we got wrapped in pretty paper, and then we sat in the dark for awhile.

One day we heard beautiful music and many busy feet and there were wonderful smells. Christmas was here. Before we knew it, we were snug around two feet. Dad said how beautiful we were and how warm and he kissed his little boy.

Then our life as socks began (repeat a few times and add action to words).

We got worn, washed, dried folded and put away,
worn, washed, dried, folded and put away.

Then something very sad happened, my twin got lost...sniff, sniff (bring out Kleenex with other hand, console and dry tears). I was very lonely, and worst of all, nobody needed me any more...sniff, sniff (more Kleenex). I would like to ask you, have you ever felt really useless? I ended up in a bag doing nothing. I wished so very much that I could be helpful, useful and kind to people.

One day Mrs. X pulled me out of a bag and transformed me into a Queen. She wanted me to be the Queen of kindness. I was very happy, my greatest wish came true.

I made this crown especially for all of you (bring out crown) so that whenever someone is kind they get to wear the crown in the classroom. I will come and visit you often and we can talk about nice things we can do to others. Bye-bye, see you soon.

This story is just one example of many variations of what you can say. Socks can be for a birthday too. With smaller children you can make it simpler, use any family combination, have only one crown or two -- one for the Queens and one for the Kings. Be encouraging, especially the first time, so many can have a turn. Children need to know how nice it feels to be kind, and soon kindness becomes part of the classroom or home.

Materials needed for Meet the King or Queen of Kindness

<u>Sock</u>:   Use one where everybody can see that it is a sock

<u>Puppet</u>: Dress up with pieces of felt or paper, glue a piece of cardboard where the mouth is.

<u>Crowns</u>: One small one for puppet -- 1 or 2 big ones for children, gold or yellow.
          Let the children decorate.

Reflections on Meet the King or Queen of Kindness

In a family it can be a good thing to make children aware of all the nice things Mom and Dad do. Children find it very funny when Dad gets to wear a crown because he fixed something or Mom gets to wear it because she prepared a very nice dinner. In a classroom being kind has to become second nature.

At first, children might do nice things just to get the crown, however eventually they will catch the spirit. It is of course the nicest when you catch the children unaware. You want to surprise, especially the shy children, when they are courteous, sensitive or helpful, with the crown. It happens that the crown goes from one head to another.

The story of the socks invokes feelings of happiness, sadness, frustration, uselessness and eventually satisfaction. Because you have a puppet that is talking to the children, they experience what the puppet is feeling. We want to make sure that children learn to feel for others and not grow indifferent and insensitive.

This crown can be disturbing the normal flow in a classroom also, so you might only want to do it for a week, here and there. It can be called Crown Week. Sometimes it becomes necessary in a classroom to refocus on kindness!

EMPATHY: (According to Webster's dictionary) The imaginative projection of one's consciousness into the feelings of another person or object; sympathetic understanding.

Ideas and examples for home or classroom to foster Empathy

We are surrounded by situations and experiences where we can teach and model empathy. These are basic principles of successful living. Concepts such as compassion, faith, patience, trust, honesty, cooperation, diligence and helpfulness should all be part of our daily lives and they can become the best and most memorable moments of our day. A tender moment, a gentle sensitivity, a connecting with another person, a sharing of pain or joy, etc.

Puppets and stories give great opportunities to talk about every issue under the sun. I want to share a few other ideas with you that I found very helpful in working with children.
It is very important that we can put ourselves into someone else's shoes or walk in someone else's moccasins, as our Native people say.

Old people: We can have an exercise one day to show how an old person feels who doesn't hear well, see well, walk well or has arthritis in their hands. We let the children play with earplugs, sunglasses, gloves and hobbled feet. Children will realize what it is like to be old and they will not laugh at an old person shuffling across the street. (See the Sad Elephant, Book 2, page 85).

The Little Blanket: One year we had a little girl in the classroom who had been sexually abused. She was mostly off the wall, in a bad mood and uncooperative. She didn't want to be touched so we couldn't hug or console her. We bought a nice soft little blanket in her favorite color and let her use it every day when she didn't feel very good. She could have it around her, beside her or sit on it. She used it every day, put it at her place after school and picked it up first thing when she came to school. It was her blanket and eventually everybody accepted it very well. Everyone knew that she needed this blanket. She was a completely changed girl, from then on she was able to participate and learn.

Little Hearts: I made stuffed little velour hearts for the classroom in different colors and kept them in a pretty box. Whenever someone was upset over something serious, like losing a grandparent or a pet, or getting hurt, they were welcome to take one of the little hearts to keep, hold it in their hands or put it in their pocket. We would tell them that when they squeezed the little heart, they would know that we loved them and that the hurt would go away soon. It was a very consoling thing in many situations. For smaller hurts, children would get a little heart for the day and put it back in the box at the end of class. One time a little girl who had a little heart gave it to a friend who was upset -- we were very touched. (See picture on previous page.)

Kleenex: Imagine a puppet bringing a Kleenex to a child that is crying, it works like a miracle! You can bring a band-aid too, with the puppet.

Pictures: I have collected what I call "feeling pictures". Some pictures are beautiful and speak volumes. You can see feelings of love, joy, hate and satisfaction on people's faces. There is friendship, happy families, lonely people and people that are hurt, etc.
Instead of doing the calendar and weather every morning, you could take one picture into the circle and have a discussion about it. It would teach empathy and vocabulary and would let a child get in touch with their own feelings. At the end you could hang it up in the classroom as the picture of the day or week.

Children love these discussions and it brings a closeness to any group. It opens children's eyes too, once in a while one of the children brought a picture to school for us to look at and discuss. They will look at books in a different way too.

> **There are many aspects of learning in a child's life and for an educator to model, to help a child be well-rounded and have balanced learning.**

What are some of the important ones?

1. Communication: Listening skills, to freely express oneself, verbal skills, vocabulary.

2. Compassion: To have patience, to feel for others, to act on pity, to be sensitive, know how to love and be loved.

3. Enthusiasm: Being excited, discovering, being curious, developing interests.

4. Behaviour: Courteous, respectful, trustworthy, honest, be pleasant.

5. Humour: See the funny side of life, laugh a lot, loosen up, let others laugh.

6. Attitude: Be an optimist, be positive, be grateful, be content, pursue inner peace.

7. Creativity: Have a good imagination, make interesting pictures in your mind, practice ingenuity.

8. Innocence: Keep your innocence but don't be gullible or a pushover.

9. Determination: Have goals and a vision, know what you like and what you are good at.

10. Common Sense: Seek sound practical judgement, have a healthy understanding of consequences.

11. Work Practices: Learn to persevere, master skills, follow instructions, learn problem solving, have confidence.

As Children see it:

STORY & PEOPLE PUZZLES

Puzzles in this Section:

1. The Christmas Tree
2. House with Family
3. Family Tree Puzzle
4. The Clown
5. Benjy and the Apple Tree
6. Old MacDonald

1. The Christmas Tree Puzzle

2 layers, 1/4" (6 mm) plywood

Precut:

- 6" by 7" (15 x 18 cm) - one piece 1/8" (3 mm) plywood.
- 6" by 7" (15 x 18 cm) - two pieces 1/4" (6 mm) plywood.
- Four pieces of molding as in Box 2, page 107 and cut down to fit the 3 pieces of plywood. Frame can be a little higher.

Trace the Christmas tree with all the pieces onto one of the 1/4" sheets and cut out the tree with a drill start (instructions in Book 3, Page 14). Trace the present onto the other 1/4" sheet. Here you do not have to do a drill start. Start cutting from the bottom and you will only see a little cut which you can fill in with glue and sand over. When you cut out the present, do not try to make a perfect square, rather, leave it a little crooked with different looking corners, so that the children will be able to put it together easily. Next, trace baby Jesus onto the 1/8" bottom sheet. As you put the squares on top of each other, you will see exactly where you can put the crib. Sand the inside of the tree and the present, then glue the squares together. Now sand the outside of the three sheets together and glue the molding on, holding it together with an elastic. Next you are ready to cut the tree and the present into pieces. Sand well and paint. I used an eraser at the end of a pencil to make the decorations on the Christmas tree. Design your own decorations! With this puzzle, I wanted to show the real meaning of Christmas. Instead of dumping out the puzzle, children like to take out the pieces of the tree first and then they can open the present to find Jesus in the manger. You can keep this puzzle with your Christmas things and bring it out during Advent.

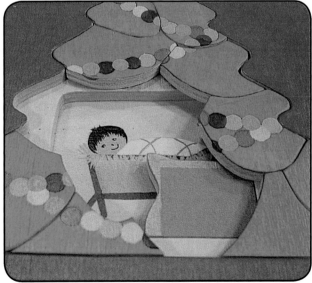

(Note: Enlarge pattern by 20%)

2. House with Family Puzzle

(add pictures of your family)

1 layer 1/4" (6 mm) plywood
Precut:

- 9 ½" by 11" (24 x 17 ½ cm) - one piece 1/8" (3 mm) plywood
- 9 ½" by 11" (24 x 17 ½ cm) - one piece 1/4" (6 mm) plywood
- 9 ½" by 11" (24 x 17 ½ cm) - one piece poster board

Trace the pattern onto 1/4" sheet. Make a drill start (instructions in Book 3, Page 14) along the house. Cut out the house, trees and the moon. Sand the inside of the frame and cut the house into pieces. Put 1/8" sheet of plywood, poster board and 1/4" sheet of plywood on top of each other. Take out windows and trace window openings onto the poster board. Cut out the windows on the poster board with an exacto knife and glue the photos behind the windows. Glue the poster board with the photos onto the 1/8" sheet of plywood. Next, the frame of the puzzle can be glued on top. Drill holes into the windows and insert small pieces of dowel so that the children can take out the windows easily. Sand everything really well and paint. Children are very attracted to a puzzle like this, especially if their own picture, their families or their friends are in the windows. This puzzle makes a nice family gift. You can com-

bine pictures of your family and the family that you give the puzzle to in the house. It would be a gift from "our family to your family." These gifts are very meaningful and last a lifetime. You could glue other pictures in the house after a while and it would be like a new toy. You can design your own house or you can add a dog house with a picture of your dog in it. I cut every window differently on purpose. If they all look the same, the children will try to jam in the pieces and so break the puzzle. You can make smaller houses, bigger houses, or a big highrise with a large family.

63

(Note: Enlarge pattern by 20%)

3. Family Tree Puzzle

(Add pictures of your family and pets)

2 layer 1/4" (6mm) plywood

<u>Precut:</u>   Enlarge pattern 20%, add 5/8" (1.5cm) frame all around. This will be the size of your puzzle. Cut one 1/8"(3mm) and two 1/4" (6mm) plywood. Cut the same size posterboard.

<u>Drill Holes:</u> My dowel pieces have a thickness of 14/32" (12mm).

<u>Dowel:</u>   On the house, drill holes the size of your dowel and on the tree a little bigger. Length of dowel 1/2" (13mm).

- Trace the pattern onto both pieces of plywood, clamp both boards together and drill the holes through both pieces at the same time with the smaller drill (size of dowel). This way you know that they are in the right spot. Drill the holes of the tree a little bigger after.

- Top layer (tree) - Cut out frame with a drill start (see Book 3, page 14). The background of the house will be the frame for the house puzzle. Here you don't need a drill start because both frames will get glued onto the 1/8" bottom sheet. Cut up both puzzles into pieces.

- Trace windows onto posterboard and cut out with an exacto knife. Glue photos behind into windows, glue posterboard with photos onto 1/8" plywood sheet. Sand frames on the inside and paint them. Glue house frame on, then the last frame for the tree puzzle. Hold all layers together with clamps, let dry. Now you can sand the outside of finished frame and all the pieces. Touch up the outside of the frame with paint. Paint all pieces including pegs (red for apples). Glue in the pegs.

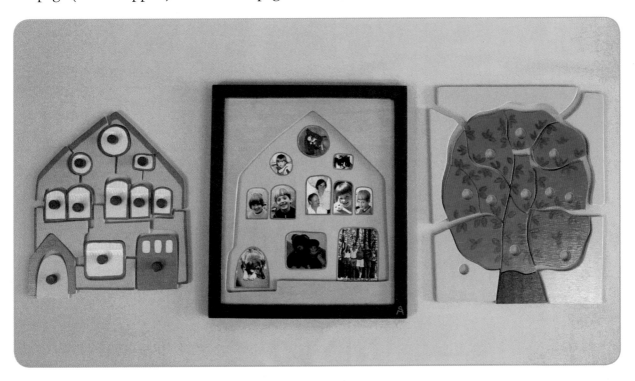

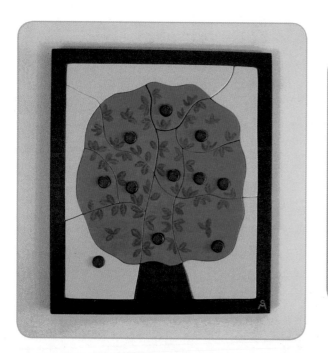

As you can see in this puzzle, the pegs of the windows become the apples in the tree.

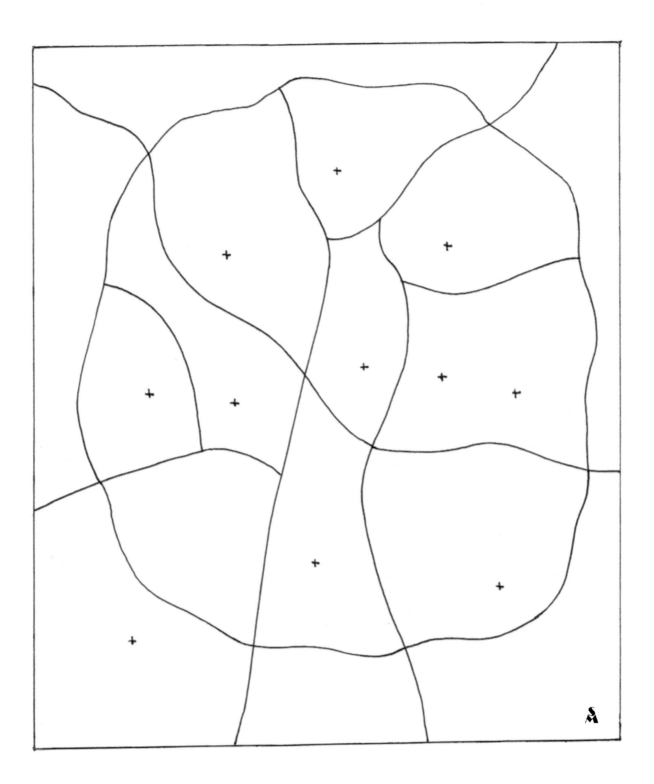

(Note: Enlarge pattern by 20%)

(Note: Enlarge pattern by 20%)

4. The Clown Puzzle

5 layer Puzzle Box - 1/4" (6 mm) plywood

Precut: 3" by 3" (7 ½ x 7 ½ cm). 5 squares of 1/4" plywood

Box: on bottom sheet 1/8" (3 mm) plywood - 4 pieces of molding.

Trace the pattern onto squares, cut pieces on the saw, sand and paint. This clown comes out of the box, has to be assembled and all folds back into the box. There are only 22 pieces in all and 14 of these are used for the clown. The yellow pieces are just background. You can copy this pattern sheet and let the children cut out the clown, color it, and paste it on a piece of paper. You can see how many different ways the clown can be set up and everyone can choose their own colors.

69

5. Benjy and the Apple Tree Puzzle

Puzzle made from a Poem. One layer ½" (12 mm) plywood

<u>Precut:</u> 11 1/8" by 8 ¼" (28 x 20 ½ cm)
- one piece ½" (12 mm) plywood
- one piece 1/8" (3 mm) plywood

This is another action puzzle that the children can play with. I made it with ½" plywood so that all the figures can stand up. It is not a puzzle in the traditional sense, because I have discarded all the excess pieces that were not needed. I designed it so that there is very little waste and that the lines are the same for the touching pieces so that it is easier for the children to put together. I have also painted all the figures on the bottom of the box because the figures are painted on both sides and so it is difficult to know how to put it together. Just tracing the pieces onto the bottom of the box would be helpful. This poem again has a lot of repetition and in addition has a nice rhythm that sounds catchy and makes everyone want to participate.

When children play on their own, they are encouraged to remember the sequence. It strengthens verbal skills, small motor skills, skills in co-ordination and creative thinking. Because both sides of the puzzle are painted, I have painted them so that the children know which side is the front. For example, I only decorated the front of the flowers or painted a little spider on the front of the tree. I wrote the name of our dog on the front of the doghouse. I even made a little cut out for the tree in the frame so that the children know where to start. With little ideas like this you can make it much less frustrating for the children and at the same time it becomes more special. Here again, I have made a drill start to cut out the frame. However, this time you can use a larger drill because you are discarding the inside squares of the ladder and the tree stand. The apples on the other hand, need a drill start (instructions Book 3, Page 14). This puzzle is a lot of work, first to prepare the wood and then to paint the pieces all around and on the bottom of the box as well. However, it is so satisfying - imagine how many hours we just watch TV! Often these are unintelligent, meaningless, low-standard type shows where we do nothing but fill in time!. I was trying to say it nicely. I feel very strongly about this issue!

The poem goes like this:

1. Farmer Bill sent Benjy out to shake the apple tree. But Benjy didn't shake the tree ...the apples didn't fall.

2. So Farmer Bill sent his dog out to go and bark at Benjy. But the dog didn't bark at Benjy. Benjy didn't shake the tree...the apples didn't fall...

3. So Farmer Bill sent his rooster out to go and peck the dog. But the rooster didn't peck the dog. The dog didn't bark at Benjy. Benjy didn't shake the tree...the apples didn't fall...

4. So Farmer Bill sent his cat out to go and scratch the rooster...But the cat didn't scratch the rooster. The rooster didn't peck the dog.

The dog didn't bark at Benjy. Benjy didn't shake the tree...the apples didn't fall...

5. So Farmer Bill sent out his cow to poke the cat with her horns. But the cow didn't poke the cat. The cat didn't scratch the rooster. The rooster didn't peck the dog. The dog didn't bark at Benjy. Benjy didn't shake the tree...the apples didn't fall.

6. So Farmer Bill went out himself to get the
   crew to work,
   so the cow poked the cat,
   the cat scratched the rooster,
   the rooster pecked the dog,
   the dog barked at Benjy,
   and the apples finally fell!

(Note: Enlarge pattern by 20%)

6. Old MacDonald Puzzle

Puzzle made from a Song. One layer ½" (12 mm) plywood

<u>Pre-cut</u>:
- 10 ½" by 8 ½" (26.5 x 21.7 cm) - one piece 1/2" (12 mm) plywood
- 10 ½" by 8 ½" (26.5 x 21.7 cm) - one piece 1/8" (3 mm) plywood

This puzzle is again an action puzzle where children can play farm. If you have a small bag with pieces of wood to be used for fences, children can make different compartments for the animals. You could simply cut up sticks from bushes to be used for this purpose. They would really have the look of a natural fence. Of course it is important to sing the Old MacDonald song. You can line up the animals as you sing. Be inventive when it comes to the ostrich or the lady bug. You can all have some giggles over those ones. Children love to do the fish because you do not hear a sound, you just open and close your mouth. This puzzle has been made similar to the Benjy puzzle, but it does not have all the difficult drill starts. On this puzzle again, you can drill a larger hole for your saw to cut out the frame. This is what you call a barn full of animals!

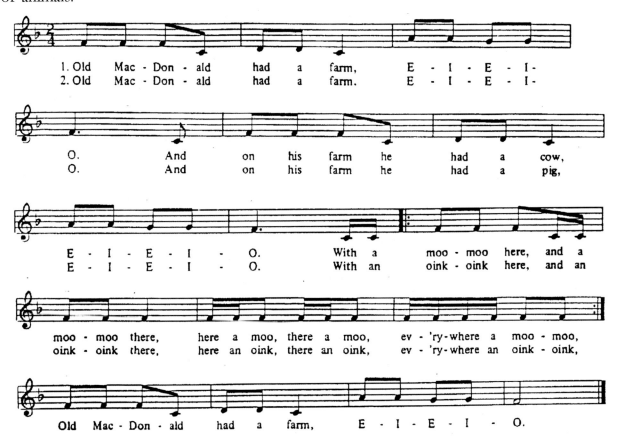

(as above, repeating each animal in reverse order).

3...and on his farm he had a duck...etc...with a quack quack here...etc.
4...and on his farm he had a horse... etc...with a neigh neigh here...etc.

Other animals to use: donkey - goose - rabbit - mouse - hen - rooster - fish - cat - ostrich
dog - llama - two birds - sheep - goat

Add a frame of
1/2" (12mm)
all around the pattern

(Note: Enlarge pattern by 20%)

PLAYROOMS and PLAYTIME

Now that you have seen the puzzle section, we need to talk about playrooms. We have to create the right space for certain toys. A large toy box where you can throw everything in, is not suitable for many toys. If you want to get into educational toys, you will have to create the right environment for them first. It can be very frustrating if you buy a beautiful, expensive toy or make something yourself with excitement and love and then see it all over the floor with pieces missing or broken. A toy loses its teaching power if it is not complete and not properly cared for. A playroom is almost like a kitchen, a work area where you can spend many hours and where everything has its place so that you can find an item when you need it. As our bodies need different foods to keep healthy and balanced, so our minds and souls need different activities to keep healthy and balanced. If children watch a lot of TV or play a lot of games on the computer without parental guidance, the children grow up very one sided and will not get the stimulation and opportunity to learn what is required for a healthy and balanced development.

Today, children often have too many toys. It seems that a playroom needs to look like a circus, be action packed and filled with material excitement. There is little room for reflection and quiet learning or time to marvel and discover things. Children get bored because this madness has no substance. If there is no food for the soul and the mind, integrated into play as well as a good, caring, loving, interaction with caregivers, children are unattached, feel insecure and then are in danger of falling into unhealthy activity seeking.

Your first step will be to create a proper play area. This in itself can be a place to practice discipline. This discipline can teach organization, and with a little bit of organization, you can work much better. Many children love order and function much better.

When our children were young, I designed and built a shelf with boxes for the toys. All the items were easily reachable for the children. The large boxes had casters on the bottom so that they could be easily wheeled around to wherever the children wanted to play. In these boxes we kept things like building blocks and the train sets. You could also use containers and plastic baskets to keep things in. For the smaller items, I covered small tins with mactac and marked them with pictures. Other shelf space was used for toys of the week or the month. This may sound like a preschool set up, but I think that it is especially important for a home where children have to keep busy and keep their minds stimulated for many more hours. If you just spend fifteen minutes a day thinking creatively about how you can occupy the children with materials and toys, it will be well worth it.

In order to keep the children interested I kept changing toys around, putting some away for a few weeks, and arranging a few toys in a different corner to create a new space. If you have something interesting already when they get up, you can start the day out right. There is less whining and attention getting and you can do your own work beside them as they play. Do not have the TV on when they get up, instead start them on something else right away.

I think raising children is the most interesting and rewarding challenge. You can never be bored and you have to be on your toes all the time to keep your creative thinking going. Make it a challenge and make a decision to enjoy it because it is really incredibly rewarding. I do not know of any job that is more important than raising our next generation.

A toy room doesn't always have to look perfect, but a clean-up time before supper helps to keep order. Once in a while we would make a group effort and all go into the playroom and do a good cleaning job. You cannot help getting things mixed up once in a while. It should not be a frustrating job, but rather an enjoyable one. In our family, toys were always treated with importance and respect. If something really nice was built, the children could leave it standing for Dad to see when he got home, or they could even leave it for a few days in order to add to it or explore new ideas and constructions. I often took pictures to give it the importance that it deserved. I decided to add a few of these pictures in the book and share them with you. This way you can see the things I am explaining..

Once you realize how important toys are and have made up your mind on how you want to handle issues of discipline, and are actively involved in creating your children's spare time, you are well on the way to an incredibly meaningful period of your life.

Playtime!

Not only do we have to prepare play areas, but we have to prepare or create the right atmosphere for play. This can already start in the crib. We should teach infants to be on their own sometimes and not always rush in when they wake up or when we hear the first sounds. I think it is important that we give children time to wake up slowly. Let them look around or play with their hands and make them feel comfortable in their own company for a while. I always tried to hold back if I could see that they were occupied in thought or in play. This also has some egotistical motives to it! I always needed time to myself, and in this way we respected each others space. I think it is important that children learn early on that we have our work to do too and that we can do this side by side. By us respecting their time and space, they learn to respect ours.

If I had to work in the garden, I would set up a playpen close by in an interesting spot with shade and a blanket so that the children could not eat the grass or the dirt. I never gave them the feeling that they had to be in the playpen but rather that they had this incredible spot to play in. It is best to include them in your activities if possible (raking the leaves, putting out the washing, sitting on a swing, etc.)

One of the pitfalls of today's society is the constant rush we are always in and all the activities that we try to cram into one day. I don't know why we think that we have to involve the child in umpteen things and be on the road constantly, often disrupting mealtimes. Our very best days were the ones where we could just stay home. The children could get into lengthy projects and be immersed in play. I think that we have forgotten how to "just be." We need constant entertainment and activities... or do we?

When I listen to parents complaining about busy schedules, mad rushes, and no time for themselves, I wonder who makes their schedules. Has our imagination gone so bad that we cannot picture how busy a week will look like if we sign up for this, that and the other? We really have to determine what is important to us as a family and as individuals. Make some sacrifices here and there and desperately try to have some sanity time at home. In this time and age where everyone wants to be liberated, let us at least be liberated from too much activity. Slow down - enjoy life more. A lifestyle or routine where you make time for educational play will pay off in the later years when children have homework and are used to working on projects. It is a small step to then exchange the excitement of play for a school project.

Water, Sand and Playdough

There is a lot to be said about the calming qualities of playdough, sand and water play. If you can make these available periodically, it is very beneficial for everyone. You do not need fancy containers, you can find old buckets, bottles, and funnels around the home. Small, old swimming pools with a hole can be used for a sand box. High buckets of water are dangerous because small children can fall in, but can't get out. Always consider the safety of the child first. Have a cover for sandboxes to keep the cats out.

These materials are loved by most children, have a theraputic quality, stimulate creative thinking and teach concepts in math, science and social skills and...are most definately worth the mess.

RECIPE FOR PLAYDOUGH

2 cups flour	2 cups water
1 cup salt	4 tsp. cream of tartar
2 teaspoons oil	food coloring

Combine in a saucepan. Cook over medium heat until it becomes a solid mass. Remove and let cool. Remember to keep covered when not in use.

Let the children play on their own as much as you can. If you can play with them, read to them or do crafts with them, that is great. Just do not disturb them all the time. Let your ears and eyes be tuned into their play, then you'll know where they are, what they are doing and how their mood is towards each other. You'll get the feeling of when to step in and when to give a guiding hand. Sometimes with one suggestion, you can extend their play time for another hour. You can help them work out their squabbles, rather than doing it for them. Often when one of them would come and complain, I'd say, "I think you can work it out," or if something was more serious I would ask them both to come and we'd see what we could resolve. Often, they would work it out themselves because they knew that I would get the other side of the story! Ha Ha!! Sometimes you may have to separate them. Do not make an issue out of this, rather let them know that they just need time on their own and that later they will enjoy each other's company again. A lot of outside play is also important; don't forget the soap bubbles.

Art Projects

Artwork is another activity that contributes to later schoolwork habits. It is very exiting to watch the child's development in drawing. They don't just scribble, they express their understanding. A child draws what he or she knows, not what they see. This way, you get a peephole into their development. I remember how excited we were when one of the children made a discovery of drawing a tummy, not just arms, legs and a head. These are milestones that need to be celebrated. We don't have to teach them to draw tummies, we can point them out in the bathtub.

It is most exciting, however, when they find it themselves.

Have paper and art materials ready all the time. Set up inviting little areas that are ready to go. Display art work, have scrap books, and write the name and the dates on the pictures. Coloring books are fun once in a while, but are quite useless otherwise. Encourage free art work because this is real expression. Someone could make a paint easel that could circulate among friends. You don't need one all the time. Have scissors and glue available according to age. Collect cardboard rolls and all kinds of different objects in a box for rainy day projects. Call it the happy box!

This is a page from Nisha's baby book where you can see the stages in learning to draw a person. All children go through similiar steps. First the person is drawn without a tummy, with legs and arms coming straight from the head. Then a tummy is added with arms still coming from the head. Next the arms are drawn from the tummy and soon children add hair, fingers, toes, etc.

Snack time can break up a boring moment or a bad mood. Pack snacks into a paper bag with a happy smile on it or let the children take the lunch box to a special place. You can arrange banana slices with raisins on top or make a star with carrot sticks or celery etc. There is always a special way to have an old snack. Cut down on pre-packaged foods. Low or no sugar foods are part of a successful childhood.

89

Helping Around the House

When play is taken seriously, it is like working. Jobs become part of the day's activities. Helping with all the different work around the house and the garden can be fun, not to mention all the things the children learn. It is well worth letting the children help. I know that it is often difficult because it would be faster for you to do a job by yourself when they are too little. When they get older, they do not want to help as much anymore. If you let them help when they are young, they will learn to job-share.

Living in a community or family has priviledges, but the work should be equally shared. There should be no question of helping, it should just be done. Often one person ends up doing most of the work and this is not good. You can do a little math by showing that a job that takes eight hours by yourself, can be done much quicker if everybody helps. If four people help, it can be finished in two hours and then everyone can do fun things together. It is good for children to feel useful and important. For regular, everyday chores they wouldn't get paid very much, but extra jobs like washing the car, doing hard garden work or helping with spring cleaning would be rewarded financially in our family.

Let all your relatives and friends know your philosophy about the importance of good toys (in a nice way), so that they all know when they give you gifts, they have to be careful. Most children are always attracted to certain toys, toys that we never allowed in the house. Our children knew this and when they got something that we didn't approve of, we would determine how much it would cost and give the money to that child to buy something of their choice. There would be a little sadness at first, but then it would turn to excitement as they realized they could go and buy something. We have to teach the children to be firm about bad influences in our life. Some things were even brought ceremoniously to a dumpster because we didn't even want to give it to any friends. It is a sensitive issue. You can explain to the child that the person meant well but you don't want to offend them. Unapproved things only came from people that we didn't know very well and so we never ran into serious trouble. From our close relatives, we would always get meaningful things. Often it is nice to add to a toy rather than getting more toys. For example, to get a new bridge or crossing for a train set will make it like a new toy. These parts are expensive, but can also be used by the next generation. Lego is great and can also be added to. Instead of another doll, we can give a new outfit to a favorite doll or simply add a new book to the library.

The social aspect can easily be brought into playtime. You can bake something for the next day's play group; you can make a picture together for grandma and grandpa; you can pick flowers for someone or make birthday cards and wrapping paper.

The building pictured below was built by Marc and Nisha for the people in our family who travel. We sent the photos of the young fire fighters to these relatives, together with a check list of what to look for and what to do in a hotel in case of a fire. Here you can also talk with the children about your own evacuation plans.

You can also teach the children early that in real relationships you also give, you don't just take. We connect the children to the big circle of the extended family. In our family this was important since all our family was so far away in Switzerland. Grandparents are especially appreciative of any attention they get from children.

Most of the pictures I took where made so that the grandparents could take part in the growing up of our children. I later realized that I was teaching the children how we wanted to be treated when we get older. A lot of people could not be bothered with spending much creative energy for their parents and are then surprised when their children leave and do the same - interesting! We always learn about financial investment, but the same thing goes for emotional investment! No money, no interest, no kindness, no kindness in return.

There should always be a good mix of different activities:

- outside play
- floor play
- table toys
- group play with friends
- play only with siblings
- play alone
- interraction with adults
- structured activities
- free activities
- jobs and chores
- making something for someone

How to Make Workshops

HOW IT STARTED FOR ME

Hands on workshops are in great demand. In general, the practical learning, seems to be more neglected. Everything is based on high academics, big words in books and talks of all different kinds. However, I think we are slowly finding out that the practical has to go hand-in-hand with the theoretical learning. High schools and universities are implementing co-op programs where young adults are exposed to the real world. Isn't that wonderful! We have to find many ways of mixing the practical with the theoretical.

Often when I go to conferences, people go from one talk to another and then when they come to my workshop, they are happy to get the practical along with the theory. So I hope, that many of you reading this book will be able to put workshops together for other people. I will try and go through some of my experiences and try to help you get a faster start and eliminate some of the pitfalls that are so time consuming. If you already have the tools, a good understanding of the different materials, and have many ideas yourself, you might be the person to consider giving workshops. You don't have to start with many different projects. One theme and three to four different projects would be enough to start.

During the years that I was at home with the children and they were in the earlier grades, a few friends and I would take turns hosting small workshops for each other. It was a very meaning-ful time as we were able to share in fellowship and create something nice. We felt connected, shared our joys and problems, complimented each other and went home enormously satisfied and injected with a new strength for the rest of the week. I think that everyone should belong to a group where they can do things together and share. You could be a person to start something like this. If you think that you do not have the place for it, or that you are not the right person, I say, "fiddlesticks!" With a few cookies, a welcoming attitude and one little project, you can do it. You can even do it with only one friend.

Remember to be practical and try not to outdo each other, especially in those busy years when the children are little. Everyone could bring their own lunch or someone else could bring the cook-ies instead of the person who is hosting. You know how it is, you will be busy cleaning up before people come. If something doesn't work, discuss it, there is always a way. It should not cost an arm and a leg. We did many projects with things we collected; choosing scraps of all kinds.

For example: self collected dry flowers and cones for wreaths and arrangements; pressed flowers and leaves for card making and pictures; knitting; embroidery; crocheting; dolls and puppets; doll clothes; Christmas things; small wooden projects; baking and cooking etc. There are many activities that you can think up on your own.

I got together with a good friend of mine and her two children once a week for the whole day. One of us would host the day, prepare the lunch and the activity. We raised our family with grandparents, aunts, uncles, nephews and nieces living far away in Switzerland, so we had to create a family in Canada. Our two families were a family for each other. We loved those days, all became very close and we two moms shared many things - and still do! It is especially important for women to be able to get together and share ideas, joys and problems. In the old days, women would meet at the water fountain or the washing hole. They would do a lot of activities together. I even think that it is important for men to get together and build sandboxes, tire swings etc. for the children. In the old days, men hunted and did fieldwork together. Someone has a saw, and someone else has a truck to get the sand. All we need now is a shovel and some muscles!! Days like this can be wonderful for families. Instead of living isolated like we often do today and simply grabbing a video, you could camp in each other's yards, or go to a campfire. I see that I am getting off topic, but life is one great experience where everything influences whatever we do.

Workshops for Larger Groups

The early projects have taught me a lot of things for my workshops, such as how much to prepare ahead of time and how certain things work for beginners. When you have a workshop for 20 people or more (25 is my upper limit), it is good to be well prepared. In the beginning, I would have baskets with all different materials and precut pieces for people to take as they were required for certain projects. That didn't work because it became too expensive. People didn't only take what they needed, they took everything there was. Sometimes, there was a run for things, a frantic grabbing - you learn as you go! Then I started the plastic bag idea. You put everything into a

bag, down to the sandpaper, thread and needle, instruction sheet, felt, fur or leather, lace or ribbon and the main pieces of wood. I would have up to forty different projects and you could easily identify the project through the plastic bag. I would only bring 10-15 different projects to a workshop, depending on the theme. This is a very easy method and it works great. The people select a project, sit down at a table and start. The confusion is cut down enormously this way. Everybody gets busy right away and they always seem to know what to do since I would have the finished product as a sample to view. Everybody enjoys workshop times, it is like therapy. Everyone sits around, makes something, uses their hands creatively and can talk with others or just work silently.

I have had many people who were surprised to find out that they could make nice things themselves. Some get so excited about their own creativity, that they get started on all sorts of projects. This is really what makes it worthwhile for me, to see that I can make a difference in someone's life. I try to make sure that projects can be finished in the timeframe of the workshop. Some people seem to have unfinished projects at home forever. However, I encourage everyone to finish things or, of course, to make many of the projects at home with their own ideas and materials. Often I work with people who are working full time or are busy students. They always appreciate the preparing I do. In earlier workshops I brought my table scroll saw for people to cut out pieces themselves. It was good for them to see how easy it is to work on a saw. With small groups it works well, especially if you have an extra room to set up the saw so there would be no noise or sawdust in the same room. However, with large groups it is sometimes very difficult. People seem to wait forever for their turn and then the saw works for hours on end and the motor burns out too quickly. Due to this, I started to precut pieces at home. I would cut for half an hour here and there, always with ear protection and a dust mask. I would keep my supplies stocked up, so when I had a workshop, I could just take things and go.

How to Save Wood

When I design the characters to be cut out of wood, I tailor-make them as much as possible and arrange them in such a way to get the least amount of scrap wood leftover. It is nice to arrange them in strips since it is hard to work with large pieces of wood under a scroll saw. If you use the same line for two pieces, you're cutting down on the wear-and-tear of your saw. (See next two Pages)

What Kind of Person do you have to be to put Workshops Together?

I have developed patterns and ideas over a long period of time and have provided tips on how to do a workshop. However, there are many other things to consider, depending on what size of workshop you plan on doing. Small workshops with only a few people and only one or two projects can work for anyone. Do not be discouraged. It is a great thing to do and I would encourage anybody to try it. To do workshops on a larger scale you need a lot of space; you have to be a collector, have an understanding family, a keen eye for suitable material that is reasonable in price, patience and long hours of preparation time. Sometimes I would meet people at my workshops that had these qualities along with excitement and a love for children!

Often I would have an assembly line of parts and materials from one end of the house to the other. I have about three rooms to myself, one being the workroom with a large table, sewing machine, table scroll saw, table drill and two walls of shelving. Another room consists of sample toys and more materials. The last room is for my portable workshop with

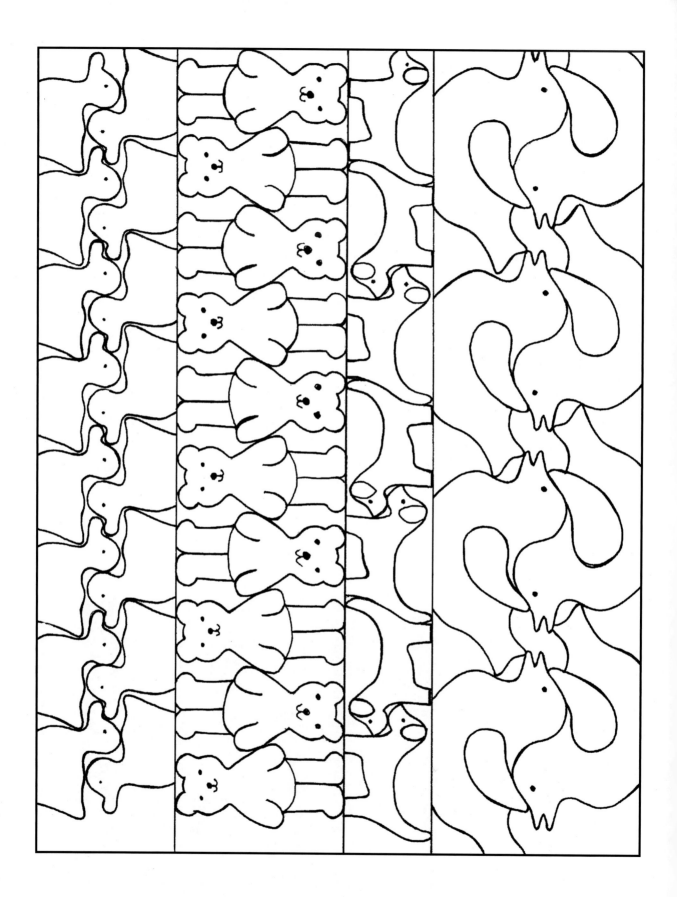

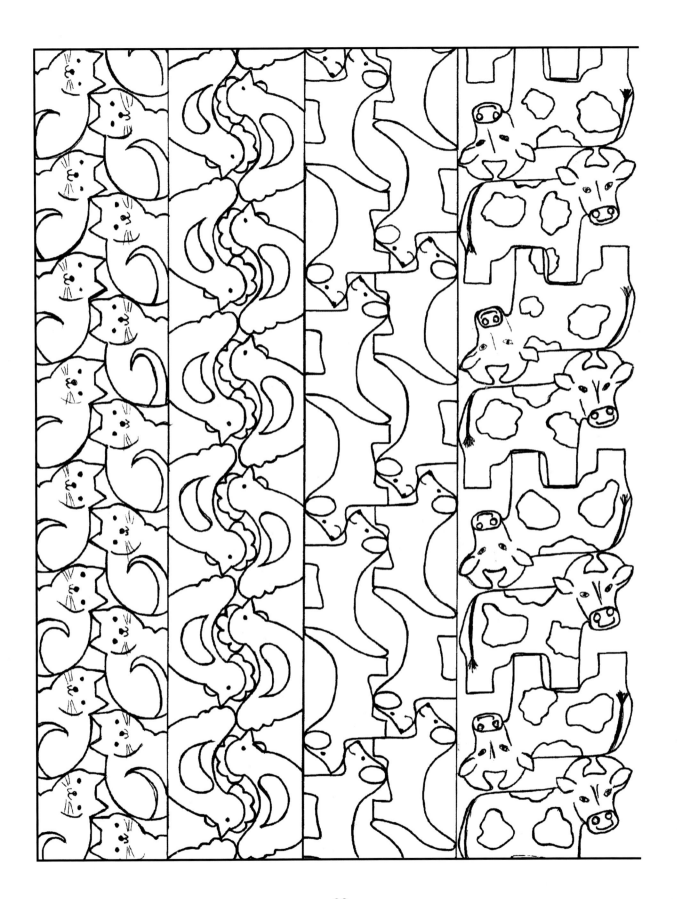

containers, sheets of wood, boxes of shells, hay, moss, logs etc. You never know what you might find in there! In addition, I use a long hallway to assemble the different materials for each package. In my case it was important for me to have a lot of different materials and scraps available. If I had an idea, I was able to put it together right away. I would try to make use of what I had rather than going out and buying something new. There are always a few different ways of doing one thing. Often I would buy inexpensive items at the dollar store, garage sales, thrift or liquidation stores. I would see the potential of an item right away, even if I did not know exactly what it would become. Eventually, however, I would make it into a story, a magnetic toy or a puppet. For example, once I found 100 wicker elephants that were very cheap because I took all of them. They eventually became the "Sad Elephant" story. Another time I found 200 birds nests for "Where is my Mommy," and the tin coaster plates for the magnetic faces. Many of these items become quite useful after much thinking at home. This is how I also kept the prices down. If you make up a story first and then try to find the materials, it will be much more expensive.

If you need to earn a lot of money or have to support a family, then hosting workshops would not be enough. It is great as a supplement to another salary or to do on the side, especially as a caregiver or ECE teacher. If you charge too much, you will not be able to sell to the less fortunate students, families or childcare centers who are trying to make ends meet. You have to cover the cost of materials and get a little money for your work. I always think that I am doing it instead of watching TV. This makes it seem worthwhile and I enjoy it more. I charge $7.50 Canadian per package (Year 2010). I charge the same amount for all the different packages. This makes it much easier. Some have more value and some have less, but all become a toy in the end. The value lies not in the material but in the potential of the toy for the child.

The Workshop

I give many different kinds of workshops, depending on who I give it to, what type of group it is, how much time I have and what the special requests are. I have:

- Whole day workshops where people make more than one project.
- Half day workshops.
- Presentations for 1 to 3 hours where people do not make a project.
- Story basket workshops.
- Puppet workshops.
- Magnetic workshops.
- Music workshops.
- Math workshops.
- Workshops where I bring a bit of everything.

At every workshop, I first give a presentation for about two hours. Here I introduce the theme, show all the samples and explain what each toy's educational learning potential is. I talk about what the children can learn as they play and about the pedagogical and philosophical values that are part of the child's development. In general I try to display an enthusiasm in working with children and an excitement in finding new ways to stimulate the children to learn with educational toys. If people come away from a workshop with the conviction that they can make a difference in a child's life, then I have succeeded. Sometimes, when we have time, I like to let people play with and discover one toy for themselves and then tell the group what they have discovered and what the child might learn with this specific toy. This type of learning is very valuable since we learn best when we discover it for ourselves. If you have just one theme, you can go into more detail and bring more examples. You can have interesting discussions where people share their experiences.

If you have the same group a few times, I would divide the themes. At the end of the presentation, I always present the story basket, especially the ones I have brought to be made at the workshop.

- We have a question and answer session.
- I show the projects that I have brought to be made.
- I explain about the different materials.
- Show a few important steps on how something should be made.
- Talk about how much things cost and the methods of payment.
- Then everyone chooses a project and later on a second one, if there are any leftover. You want everyone to have a good choice for the first project.

Once everyone is working, I just float around and give a helping hand if necessary. It is usually a good idea to sit people together who are making the same project because I can keep the finished product at that table. This way, when I explain something, everyone can listen and can help each other. I encourage people to walk around and look at all the other projects. This gives them the confidence that they could have made any of them.

At the end, I ask everyone to help clean up and put things into their proper places. It is amazing how some people can walk away and leave a huge mess. There are usually the same people who feel obliged to help and will make sure that everything is left the way we started. They too are usually the ones who help me carry everything back to the car. How wonderful it is to have this group of people nicely sprinkled everywhere. What would we do without them? I always pack my toys myself so that I am sure that everything is complete and ready for the next workshop.

Different Projects I Bring to Workshops that are included in this Book Series

1. Stories:
The Horse and his Hat
The Little old Lady
The Sad Elephant
Peter the Fisherman
Color story
Rosy and Posy
The Grasshopper and the Bug
Your Own Special Story
Grow a Pumpkin
Ocean
Two Owls
The Village
The Little Valentine
The Princess and the Frog
The Flower that Smiled
Noah's Ark
The Fox and the Crane
The Thirsty Bird
Sun and Wind
5 Little Ducks
5 Little Bunnies

2. Math:
Small Math Box
Heart Puzzle
Hammering game
Felt Board

3. Magnetic Toys:
Fishing Game
Magnetic Fruit Trees
Magnetic Faces
Matching Game

4. Puppets:
Hand Puppets
Finger Puppets
Cone Puppets
Broomstick Dolls
Squeeze my Cheeks Puppet
Tumble Fritz
Glove Puppets
Dress Doll
Climber
Athletic Clown

Plus new stories and toys I designed and added to my collection

Other math projects are included in stories, magnetic toys or puppet sections. For example: The ocean story where you have different sizes of shells and count to ten; the village story with different numbers; and counting five little ducks or bunnies. All magnetic toys have either counting, matching, or sorting that can be used for math concepts.

How to Arrange a Workshop

- Arrange date, time frame and fee.
- How many people will be there? 20-30 is a good number depending on space, but smaller groups are great too!
- What theme you will have?
- Background of people attending? (students, parents).
- How large is the room?
- How many tables are available?
- Where is the closest water?
- How far do you have to carry your stuff? Is there help?

All the rest of the preparation time is done at home.

I usually have about five large containers with good handles:

- 1 is filled with all my sample toys of things we will make
- 1 is for toys that are purely for presentation.
- 1 is for the basket stories I will present.
- 1 with all the prepackaged projects ready to go.
- 1 with materials to set up paint tables, extra materials like felt, fur, fabric, thread and scissors, glue and other tools.

I usually get there about a half an hour early to get set up. If I am lucky, I will get Nisha to come and help me. Nisha is a teacher also and I'm very happy to get her help. We first set up the tables and chairs. I have two tables at the front for all my finished toys and I arrange the chairs close around me so that everyone can hear and see well because many of the pieces are small. You can determine how many paint tables you need and how much space to work on as well. I use old plastic table cloths for the paint tables. After the room is arranged, I set up the tables and group things according to theme:

- Puppets
- Magnetic toys
- Stories
- Math related toys and other puzzles

This way you know right away where to find things as you talk.

Mostly I travel with my car, but every so often I get invited to other provinces or isolated communities in British Columbia where I then fly. Then my containers are all packed like puzzles to fit all the materials I need. I enjoy very much going to smaller communities, then I have librarians, speech pathologists, teachers, ECE workers, leaders from First Nations groups, parents and crafts people all in one session. These people usually know each other and have a nice time as we work on projects and share ideas.

Often I go to schools, child-care centres and libraries to tell stories to the children. This is always very special.

Who Could Benefit from these Workshops?

1. E.C.E Students (Early Childhood Education)
I have been giving many of my workshops to E.C.E classes at the college level. I feel that all E.C.E programs should have these types of workshops included in their curriculum. This is where students see the practical coming together with the theoretical. It often gives them a badly needed shot of excitement as they are trying to cope with heavy workloads and sometimes forget why they are doing what they are doing. It brings into focus the reality that they are doing all this because they love to work with children. As they go through their practicum and are able to use what they have made themselves, they can enjoy a special reward. The story baskets are especially great because the children are so glued to what is happening that the student teacher does not have to worry too much about disciplinary problems. It is very important that these first few experiences working with children are pleasant experiences for the student teacher.

2. Grandparents:
I gave my first workshop to grandmas not so long ago. This was a great experience. Grandmas, as well as the grandpas, have a lot of talents. They are the ones that have the button boxes, a piece of fur, some scrap wood in grandpa's workshop, an old broom handle and best of all, a sewing machine, a saw, a drill and other necessary tools. A few grandparents getting together to make things for their grandchildren can be very rewarding.

3. Home Schooling Parents:
It is an incredible task and commitment to home school children. Parents are always looking for new ideas and support. Many of these projects could be made by the children. Groups of parents or children or combinations of both would be great for workshops. I gave a workshop for mothers and daughters which was a great success. The girls were between 10 and 15. There are home school parent groups that are looking for hands on projects for their meetings.

4. Caregivers of Small Children:
Every community has their caregivers associations or groups where people who work in daycares, preschools or family daycare's get together. They always look for speakers or people to do workshops. They especially appreciate hands on workshops.

5. Parent Groups:
There are many different parent groups organized through school boards, churches, communities and through continuing education. Many parents are aware of the difficulties the children are facing these days and are looking for help and guidance. I have always enjoyed working with parents. There is always a special love for their children and an earnest interest to do what is best for them. It makes life so much more interesting for them to know more about their child's development and to realize what is going on in their child's mind and the learning that happens when they play.

6. Other Language Groups:
For people teaching other languages, these workshops are very beneficial, especially the story baskets. As you tell a story in another language, children can watch as you move things and talk at the same time. Together with your expression, movement and tone of voice, they will easily understand the meaning of the story.

7. Blind Children:

I have not explored this area, but I would like to one day. However, I think that many of these toys would be suitable for blind children. Since they cannot see a book, they can experience the story by touching the different characters. Comparing simple things to their own life and experiences, having a few items in a basket that they recognize, and acting out simple actions are all very helpful. A puzzle story would be nicely confined and would heighten their sense of touch.

8. Disabled Children:

People working with physically or mentally disabled children would benefit from these workshops. These children often need extra or special stimulation, something that is different and draws them out and makes them spend that extra energy to reach out. These toys will make them respond because they demand to be explored further. The children are motivated by these toys and stories and through repetition are able to master skills and tasks.

Final Tips

I never bring a project to a workshop that I have not made myself, because then I'm sure that it will work. I always have the finished toy with me. It is good to let people figure out how to complete their project by looking at the finished item. One of your first steps would be to have a little collection of toys that you can add on to, to do the presentation. If you have a few items from every section to explain about the learning steps and the child's development and you can make it really interesting, you can have everyone making the same project at the end. For example, if everyone makes a puppet, every puppet will come out differently. This is very rewarding for you to see also. I hope that many of you will find fulfillment in this kind of work. I am very fulfilled working and preparing at home and hosting a workshop once in a while. I usually come home from my workshops happy and tired. Always be prepared to find treasures wherever you go.

Tools and Materials

I should stress that I realize that not everybody who reads this book series is necessarily the type of person who will go ahead and make all the projects presented. Some readers will take the concepts which are presented and use them to buy good toys for their children, whereas other readers will go ahead and make the puzzles, puppets, etc which are presented.

However, as mentioned earlier on in this book, everybody can make the projects, and I hope that all the readers will try and complete some of the projects. Making a toy for one child or a group of children must be one of the most satisfying experiences I know. When you watch a child's face as they play with your toy and see them learn, it is priceless!

In this section I present some tips and suggestions for those readers who would like to make some of the presented projects. I have developed these over the last many years through trial and error.

I should also mention that besides purchasing the specific materials mentioned in this book from your local hobby shop, you can also use scraps of materials that you find around home. You can visit your local carpenter, furniture or model building shop for scraps. In many cases the use of scraps can lead to inspiration and creativity.

Wood

Plywoods:

I always get good quality plywood for many reasons:

1. It has less slivers.
2. It cuts nicer on the saw.
3. It is a lighter color and the paints look brighter on it.
4. It is stronger.
5. You have less waste.
6. The finished toy looks much nicer.
7. It is easier to work with.

It is worth it to pay a little more for the better quality plywood. Finished plywood that you use for toys has to be good on both sides. I always make sure that the better side is on top of the finished toy. Once you determine what quality plywood you want, you still want to check all the sheets, because they are not all the same. You can save a lot of time later when you sand and finish, if you take care when selecting the sheets. Most of the plywood sheets I use are birch wood. I use the following thicknesses:

1/8" (3 mm)	3 ply
1/4" (6 mm)	5 ply
3/8" (9 mm)	7 ply
1/2" (12 mm)	5 ply

You can get ½" plywood that is 9 ply (meaning that there are nine layers of wood glued on top of each other), but that is very hard to cut with the saw. The ½" plywood that I use has three layers of fairly soft wood on the inside. On each side there is good quality hardwood on the outside, so it is 5 ply. It cuts very nicely with the saw. I usually have the plywood sheets cut into strips at the lumber store, so that I don't have to handle large sheets. Most of the lumber stores will sell you ¼ of a sheet. When you only make a few toys, you do not need a whole sheet.

Moldings:

I use different types of moldings for the boxes. They are a good quality wood and there is a good variety. You will have to see what you can find at your lumber store. I mainly use three different types. Choose good strips without cracks or slivers.

Make sure you design your boxes a little larger than your squares. I like to have about 1/8" (3 mm) extra space. If the pieces fit too tightly into the box, it can be frustrating for the children. If there is too much space the puzzle doesn't sit nicely.

Box 1: This molding fits nine layers of plywood. As you can see it is rounded on one corner, it makes nice boxes.

Box 2: This one fits five layers and is also rounded. I cut this one down for my Four Seasons Apple Tree (Book 3, page 45). The height of this puzzle is three layers of ¼" (6 mm) plywood plus one layer of 1/8" (3 mm). For the Christmas Tree puzzle which is two layers of ¼" (6 mm) plywood plus one layer of 1/8" (3 mm), I cut it down also (see page 61).

Box 3: This molding is ideal for three layer puzzles and for larger boxes. I use this one for the hammering game box too (Book 3, pages 32 & 33).

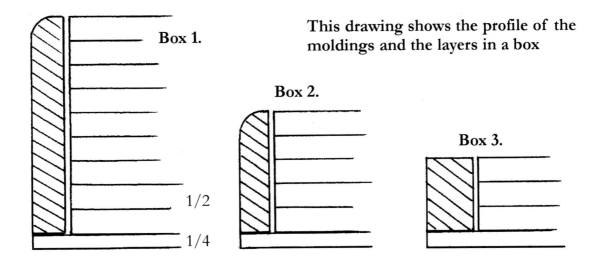

Box 1.

This drawing shows the profile of the moldings and the layers in a box

Box 2.

Box 3.

1/2

1/4

Dowels:

I used many different thicknesses of dowel for the different projects. You will see them throughout this book series with such projects as:

  * finger puppet stand
  * broomstick dolls
  * peg boards
  * flowers
  * cone puppets
  * hammer
  * handle for magnetic stage

You can buy hardwood dowel in many different diameters that are quite expensive. There are also some standard diameter softwood ones that are more reasonable.

Tools and Materials

Table saw:

I have a small table saw in the garage, where I precut all the parts for the boxes and all the squares and rectangles for the puzzles. When I set up the saw, I usually cut a few pieces at the same time. Even if you make two the same, you can save time and make nice gifts.

Fret Saw:

This is a hand saw. It is very reasonably priced and works great for ¼" and 1/8" plywood. For the first few years, I cut everything on this saw. It has a very thin saw blade (like a wire with teeth) so that you can cut tight corners.

Scroll Saw:

This is my electric saw, and I wouldn't know what to do without it. I use it in my work room, where I have everything in easy reach from my swivel chair. There are many different saws that you can buy. One thing to look for is the attachment of the saw blade. My saw has very strong saw blades with little pins already attached so that I can easily exchange them. It is very frustrating, if you have a saw on which the blades always break. It is also good to have a built in vacuum so that you do not breathe in too much sawdust. I always wear ear protection and a dust protector mask. If you do regular maintenance on the saw and do not use it for hours at a time, it will last a long time. I usually cut for about ½ hour to one hour and then do something else. Maintaining the saw means oiling it regularly and blowing out all the sawdust, especially in the motor, when it becomes necessary. You do not want it to clog up.

Paints:

I use acrylic paint in 2 fl. oz. (60 ml) bottles. I also use one or two sets of these paints for workshops depending on the class size. You can find them in stationery stores, hobby and craft stores, lumber stores, department stores etc. Shop around for a good price. There are many different brands but so far I have been able to mix them together even if they come from different companies. The consistency is usually just right for these kinds of projects. Sometimes, you have to add a little water. These paints are non-toxic and waterproof so you will never get dizzy. You can wash the brushes with soap and water. I squeeze out a bit of paint on a plate. This way you can easily mix the paints if you have to add a little white or any other color. Brush the paint on evenly (not too thick and not too thin). You will soon get a feel for how it works best. For most of the colors you only have to do one application, though white, yellow or green often need another coat. I brush the paint on with the grain of the wood. I always put the base color on first and then wait (approx. 15 min.) before I paint on the details like faces, flowers, and special lines.

Brushes:

I use soft brushes from ½" (12 mm) down to very fine ones for detail. Brushes are expensive, but if you take good care of them, you can use them for a long time. If you do not wash them right away, they get hard and are ruined. I always wash them with soapy water.

Varnishes:

You do not have to varnish these paints, but it gives it extra protection and a better finish if you do. I use water based Varathane. There are three different types; clear gloss, clear semi-gloss, and clear satin (or flat). Use the one you prefer. I mainly use semigloss and satin, but gloss looks nice also and is really good for when you have to wipe the toys with a damp cloth once in a while. I prefer brushing the varnish on. It is always a nice finishing job. If you spray varnish, make sure you do not get the pieces stuck to the newspaper.

Glue:

For all my projects I use white glue. It works especially well for wood. It bonds fast and dries clear. You can buy the white school glue; it is non-toxic and washable. I wipe excess glue off with a slightly damp cloth. For projects with photos or calendar pictures, I use glue sticks so that it bubbles less.

Putty:

If you have to fill holes in the wood, you can use Durham's water putty. It is a powder that you mix with water to the right consistency. Fill the holes, let it dry one hour, sand over it and then paint it. It sticks well and does not shrink. Sometimes there are holes in the plywood and when you cut out your pieces you come across them. This putty is good because you can mix small amounts of putty with just a few drops of water.

Nails:

Keep a small assortment of nails handy. To finish boxes, I use ½" (12 mm) finishing nails.

CHILDREN LEARN WHAT THEY LIVE

If a child lives with criticism
He learns to condemn.

If a child lives with hostility
He learns to fight.

If a child lives with ridicule
He learns to feel guilty.

If a child lives with tolerance
He learns to be patient.

If a child lives with encouragement
He learns confidence.

If a child lives with praise
He learns to appreciate

If a child lives with fairness
He learns justice.

If a child lives with security
He learns to have faith.

If a child lives with approval
He learns to like himself.

If a child lives with acceptance and friendship
He learns to have love in the World.

Kristone

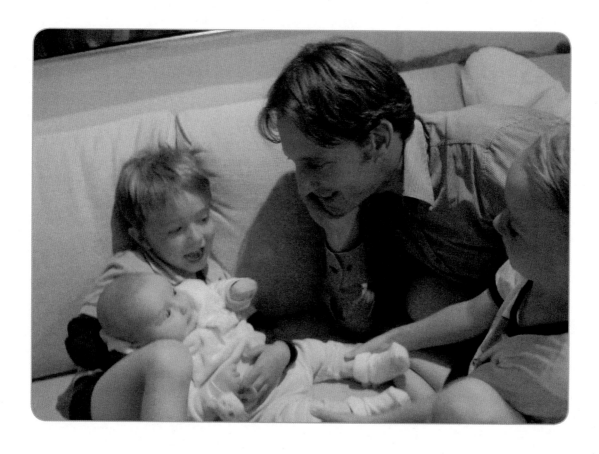

Final Thoughts

I think that empathy and compassion are more easily learned, if we first learn not to think of ourselves as being so important. I let our children know early that in our family they were loved, cherished, very special and important. But as soon as they leave the house and family, they will be like everyone else, not worth more or less, not extra special or more important than the person beside them. This is nothing more than reality! They should learn early and feel comfortable with not being the center of attention everywhere.

It makes life much easier, if we don't have to worry about ourselves so much and we learn to respect and understand people around us more.

Egotistic motives of self are predominant in our time so that we are experiencing a crisis where:

INDIVIDUALISM (me, me, me)

HEDONISM (pursuit of pleasure)

MINIMALISM (do little, gain much)

 **RULE**

So unfortunately, empathy falls mostly by the wayside.

Compassion according to Webster's dictionary: Suffering with another, sympathy, pity, consideration, an act of mercy.

Compassion:
- Is it something we either have or don't have?
- Can it be learned, grasped with our mind and heart?
- Does it have to be processed by the mind first or by the heart?
- Is bonding crucial in the baby years?
- Can it be developed and nurtured by example?
- Can we devise a means of practicing compassion in the family in education and as a society?
- Is our ego getting in the way -- are we considering ourselves too important?
- What makes us happier: Fullfilling our own desires or making others happy?
- Are our expectations of others and of life too great, and are we thinking that we are entitled to everything we want in life?

I'd like to leave you with these thoughts. In the end it all comes down to each individual. If we all wait for others to make the changes or wait until our society or times change, nothing will happen. Changes will come one person at a time. Let's have hope, courage and faith that we **CAN** make a difference!!

About the Author...

I was born, raised and got my Degree as a Kindergarten teacher in Switzerland. 40 years ago, Eric and I were married and emigrated to Canada. I worked in the ECE field ever since, either as a teacher, a curriculum designer, a conference speaker or as a Mom to Marc and Nisha, now 34 and 32. 25 years ago I started to give workshops throughout the Vancouver area to ECE workers, students and to various parent groups and worked at the local University College of the Fraser Valley part-time as a sessional in the ECE department for a few years.

Children are my passion and toys are my hobby.

After much encouragement I have finally put my ideas, thoughts and experiences into **"Learn to Play - Play to Learn."**

It is my belief that the potential within the child is much greater than we could ever imagine. **It is my hope** to make a difference for the children and to awaken a new love and excitement for all people working with children. It is truly one of the greatest jobs to raise our next generation. **It is my wish** to create an awareness that too much TV watching is not only unwholesome for children but squanders a lot of valuable time at a critical age that will never return. We **can** make a difference that will help build a good foundation for life.

I have a special love for parents who make a commitment and take child rearing seriously. If I can help put more joy, fun and at the same time some concept learning into this process for them I will have succeeded. I can boldly say I loved being a Mom. I was very privileged that I did not have to work full-time outside of the home, and was able to keep in touch with my profession.

With this book series I hope to put more importance on child rearing and encourage young mothers (and fathers) to stay at home, especially in the early years if at all possible. I am very encouraged to see a strong movement back to this and hope that eventually society will give it the importance it deserves.

The combination of my own childhood, raising our own family, the thorough education Switzerland gave me, the great opportunity Canada provided me with, as well as God's unfailing guidance brought this book about.

Susan Munzer